CU00969051

# Smile of a
# Midsummer Night

# Smile of a Midsummer Night

*A Picture of Sweden*

by
## Lars Gustafsson

and
## Agneta Blomqvist

*Translated from the Swedish by*
## Deborah Bragan-Turner

Armchair Traveller
*at the* bookHaus

First published as *Das Lächeln der Mittsommernacht*
by Lars Gustafsson and Agneta Blomqvist
© 2013 Carl Hanser Verlag München

Published in Great Britain in 2015 by
The Armchair Traveller at the bookHaus Ltd
70 Cadogan Place
London SW1X 9AH
*www.hauspublishing.com*

ISBN 978-1-909961-04-3
eISBN 978-1-909961-05-0

Typeset by MacGuru Ltd
Printed in Spain by Liberdúplex

# Contents

# *Foreword: The Map of Sweden*

This country can sometimes appear to be slightly too long. Our childhood textbooks presented a 'normal' version of Sweden, where certain trees actually produced apples and plums and where there were rivers that could be reeled off easily at the schoolmistress's command: Ätran, Niskan, Lagan, Viskan. We were approaching our thirties before we, the authors of this book with its medley of personal experiences, realised that there are rivers, in the far north to be precise, that are as wide as the Danube, wider than the Loire and as mighty as the Rhine, that they make these geography-book rivers look like pleasant little streams, fit for rowing and fly fishing.

The same could be said of the lakes, and of those there are many: on a sunny summer's day the Mälaren or the Hjälmaren is full of white sails, cement carriers and motor boats. On a similar day the Store Lulevatten or Torneträsk will feature barely a single sail and no trace of a turbulent wake.

In this respect the country is so remarkable, it isn't even known particularly well by its own inhabitants. When Carl Linnaeus set off on his royal mission to Lapland one fine spring morning in 1732, it was in fact an expedition into an unknown land – in principle the same as Peter Forsskåhl's and Anders Sparrman's journeys into foreign parts of the world.

It's not the same as in Linnaeus's day – but there is still much for the individual traveller to discover, and the authors of this book are the first to admit that it applies to them too. Research into both history and geography is far too great a task for a single lifetime. Or even for two, as in our case.

We will confine our account to personal experience, to books we have read and conversations we have had. We have taken the decision not to indicate who has written what. Our route has been from the Swedish south to the very furthest north with far-ranging excursions to the east and west and into Swedish literature. We hope the reader will enjoy our journey with us.

Very few value judgments will be found amongst these pages. But there is one that should be obvious: if we didn't think Sweden was an inspiring country in which to live, we wouldn't live here.

*Agneta Blomqvist and Lars Gustafsson*
*Säms Herrgård in Tanum Municipality, 3 August 2012*

# The Swedish South

Like a spider's web of blackness
Hang the dripping threadlike boughs.
In the silent February night-time
Singing water softly purls,
Out of valley rocks and pathways,
Floating, murmuring from a spring.

In the silent February night-time
Gently weeps the sky.

Vilhelm Ekelund, 1880–1937

The southern provinces, Skåne, Halland and Blekinge, which were incorporated into Sweden late in its history – with the Treaty of Roskilde in 1658 – and remained in dispute long thereafter, have continued in a subtle way to be foreign for those of us who come from the provinces around Lake Mälaren. And perhaps even more so for the provinces in the north.

A February night for us is normally very cold and very dark, and every field is covered in dry snow, whipped by the wind into evil swirls; in short it is *Niflheim*, the equivalent for the ancient people of the north to Hell, which was much too warm and comfortable for their purposes. In contrast, however, there are some years when the Skåne plain can find itself under the weeping clouds of a silent February night.

It is not always the case. The lowland areas between Skanör and Lund can be an inferno of snowstorms in January up to the beginning of February. Women in labour have to be ferried to maternity hospitals in all-terrain tracked vehicles, remote farms wait for days for their roads to be open again, and even then between metre-high banks of snow: walls of snow that would typically only be seen as far north as Kiruna or, conceivably, Umeå at this time of year.

Spring duly arrives. The plane from Bromma levels sharply on its approach to avoid an eagle, the captain says. Down below can be seen a flock of wild geese on their way north. There are still patches of snow here and there, while the beech forests are already beginning to change colour.

Coming to Skåne in my childhood was always rather like a trip abroad. Wild rabbits hopping and bouncing around in the fields instead of hares. Beech forests instead of pines and firs, white houses instead of Falun red, castles instead of country manors, opulent dinners in comparison to the ascetic ways of Uppsala's philosophy circles around 1958, continental philosophy instead of that of Cambridge, Oxford and Chicago. In Lund, in the fifties, people would continue their seminars in the bar of the magnificent old Grand Hotel. In Uppsala it was Kajsa's coffee shop on Drottninggatan.

In the summertime vast swathes of Blekinge and Halland can look like a garden, in contrast to the austere and sometimes extremely monotonous north European forest belt. Here there are delightful sandy beaches and seaside resorts such as Torekov and Båstad, filled with idyllic summer homes, owned mostly by an affluent upper class.

Social diversity is much stronger in the south of Sweden. There are huge farmland estates, such as Värnanäs or Simonstorp, often with a substantial chateau at the centre from the time of the Swedish empire, and there are quiet little fishing communities like Borrby and Torekov. But there are also troubled, socially isolated immigrant slums such as Malmö's Rosengård, with all the familiar problems of other similar inner-city areas in Europe.

The old thatched farmhouses, built round a square with a well in the middle, have become symbolic of this province. It should not be assumed you will find only natives of Skåne in these farmhouses; they were popular with Stockholmers as long ago as the sixties. And Dag Hammarskjöld's Backåkra has also become something of a symbol. It was to this place the UN's second Secretary-General, known to be of a contemplative nature, withdrew when he left UN headquarters.

The south of Sweden has its own literary tradition, which emerged at the turn of the nineteenth century. When August Strindberg flees from Paris, where unknown forces seem to threaten him and rule his life, he ends up with a friend in Lund and instantly recognises the peace of the industrious

3

little town. The quiet inhabitants appear completely absorbed, each and every one of them, in their own business. No one demands anything of him, and at this moment that is exactly what he needs.

'The academic farming community' is a common expression in Vilhelm Ekelund's time. A little of the old Lund milieu can still be experienced on a summer evening in our new century. The sphere in Bishop Agardh's romantic garden next to the unique Kulturen museum reflects the green of the enormous elms. The streets weave between half-timbered houses and ordinary buildings. From Maggie's attic the different roof pitches in the historic parts of town look like the dark facets of a crystal. The Grand Hotel, memorable venue for countless parties and punch-drinking evenings, stretches up towards the sky with its fake Gothic towers. And on the other side of the park the express trains to Copenhagen, for the most part all delayed, make almost no impression on the buoyant hum in the bar.

And yet there is another Lund. The town is wealthy, the house prices in the historic centre remarkably high. The large innovation industries that have grown out of the work of university laboratories block many a view over the plain. There are pharmaceuticals and software companies, not to mention the headquarters of the modern milk carton empire: Tetra Pak.

But at the heart of Lund – the word *lund* means 'grove' in Swedish and it really is a grove, probably once a place of heathen sacrifice, where the high altar was built by its spring – rises the imposing Romanesque cathedral. What first strikes the chance visitor is, of course, the astronomical clock, a monument not just to the brilliance and precision of engineering in the centuries between Fibonacci and Cardano, but also to the ever problematic issue of making a mathematical timekeeping instrument to accord with the planet's strangely imprecise annual revolutions. And, in common with many other decorative clocks in town halls and cathedrals on the continent, it has a daily procession of biblical figures moving stiffly forward beneath raised trumpets, pulled by the clock's powerful lead weights. What is a spring-driven clock, with its capricious action, doomed to be constantly corrected by cone-shaped regulators, compared to the weight-driven clock's dependable and constant mechanism, determined only by gravity, the greyest, dullest and most reliable of the four fundamental forces of nature?

The well fascinates me even more: this deep, dark well that must have been there long before Christendom, from time immemorial marking a place of worship, a holy grove.

What's down there, in the blackness?

Organisms, states a very learned little pamphlet that can now only be found in nearby antiquarian bookshops and the impressive university library: *Plant and Animal Life in Lund Cathedral*. Nothing more than organisms.

# Marshland Berries

Feeling completely at home in a country means knowing exactly what you can and cannot eat in its countryside: wood sorrel and dandelion leaves, ground elder and pine needles.

A very early exercise in reality, just like feeling and seeing your way, is *tasting* your way. You soon discover that the dark blue sloe berry, which flowers so prettily down by the shores of the Mälaren, is troublesome to your mouth, which puckers up, pinched and wrinkled on the inside, into a tiny little purse.

One particular memory of the marshlands: the smell of an old-style pharmacy emanating from the meadowsweet and mosses, the low sound of the wind in the isolated trees, the boredom of sitting in a clump of cranberries while your parents were picking.

The cranberries, hanging sparsely from frail trailing stems, were not easy to pick. Far too acidic for the taste buds if harvested before the frost, so fragile they used to break in the basket – this was the raw material for the most wonderful preserve. Perfect with game, but that was not much in evidence in the 1940s when my parents were picking mushrooms and berries and fishing for roach in Norra Nadden Lake. It was a time of hardship, when people made whatever use of nature they could.

I wouldn't realise until much later in life that these foodstuffs, like the cloudberry and the frostbitten cranberry, laboriously picked in meadows, in the remnants of charcoal kilns and out on the shifting marshes, were also delicacies. The bog bilberry has narcotic effects. If you eat more than around ten, you'll fall asleep. A jelly made from bog bilberries and served with, for example, some grilled grouse, would grace any decadent cookbook.

When I sat there among the tufts of grass, small, bad-tempered, with the impenetrable sulkiness of a seven-year-old, the berry that attracted me most was the bog bilberry. So much more mysterious than the regular bilberry, it had huge, deep blue berries and dark bluish-green leaves and didn't really seem to belong in a Nordic flora. The aroma was forever mingled with the scent of meadowsweet and moss and the earthy smells from the black water, and the taste always had something foreign, slightly disconcerting about it.

It had something of the tranquillity of a Japanese rock garden. The unfamiliar, semi-sharp, dreamlike taste brings to mind the mysteries of Taoism:

Cautious, like crossing a stream in mid-winter; observant, like moving in fear through hostile land; modest, retiring

like ice beginning to melt; dignified, like an honoured
guest; genuine, like natural, untouched wood; receptive,
like an inviting, open valley; friendly, like muddied water,
freely mixing.

Tao-Te-Ching on the Tao of the Ancients

# *The Geometric City*

The end of the seventeenth century: what a strange mixture of brutality and the thirst for knowledge that stemmed from nascent rationalism! Monsieur Descartes develops a coordinate system that provides a visual depiction of the whole of mathematics; he makes a secret study of Platonic solids – five regular, convex polyhedra with identical faces – and discovers that the sum of the vertices plus the faces minus the number of edges always equals two. Space has hidden properties which only appear when the pleats and folds are carefully considered. Newton and Leibniz introduce differential calculus and the whole business bears something in common with a sailing ship leaning perilously over. For the most part this is an age of leaning, bending, flexing and turning.

It's an age that believes in itself. The steam engine is waiting round the corner; Polhem transports gunboats through the forest to Svinesund in Charles XII's last war, his senseless campaign against Norway. New inventions such as dry docks and canal locks emerge to challenge the distinction between water and land. Sir Isaac Newton becomes Master of the Royal Mint and introduces the milled edge to every silver pound coin, a feature which pitilessly betrays whether anyone has filed any silver away for personal gain. It is the age of angular measuring instruments, chronometers and enormous clock towers.

King Charles XI decides upon the location for the base for the Swedish navy: Karlskrona. Situated on the innermost of a group of islands, it is easy to defend and an ideal position for the naval force. Sailors, stonemasons, and German craftsmen – so many of them that they will create their own German community – are brought there. It is not the only connection with German culture. When the centre of Karlskrona is rebuilt after the last great fire in the 1890s, it is in the same eclectic Berlin style as that of Södermalm in Stockholm.

In the light of a summer evening the old city looks like a stage-set by Chirico for a mystery play. The oversized square, onto which Trinity Church faces, is almost deserted: a scene in an opera, where no one has yet made an entrance or where all the singers have just left the stage. The Admiralty Clock Tower with its formal geometry reminds the visitor of an era when chronographs, sextants and logarithm tables opened up a new world. In 1686 the first battleship slides down the slipway into the shipyard. In 1690, the year of fire, the Pommern is equipped with sixty cannons. It is the age of mathematicians. And warships.

When the railway arrived from Kalmar and Växjö, Karlskrona was the end of the line. The feeling you have today is still the same as the one described by Fredrik Böök in a journey he made at the beginning of the twentieth century: you emerge from Småland's dense, scrubby, coniferous forests into a welcoming deciduous wood that has the air of a garden. All the brooks and streams are moving in the same direction as the traveller: towards the sea. And the railway station is on the main island, Trossön, more or less out on a jetty. This has been a naval port since the days of Charles XI, but nowadays the only naval vessels at the moorings are the Coast Guard's fast-response boats.

In the large maritime museum down by the harbour the visitor learns about warships, great naval battles such as the Battle of Svensksund, the bloody chaos on gun decks during combat, about shipbuilding and rigging. The tools they used, intended for working on the hardest oak, look like giants' toys. Ropes run amok in ever more complex algebraic knots. The hemp fibres grow thicker in a ranked system of blocks, from strands to rope, until they become mooring lines for warships.

A suitable formula for this age would combine one symbol for its cruelty and one for the richness of its collective mind.

The traveller goes from one island to another and scarcely notices that they are islands. They are all linked together by bridges in a single cohesive unit that has something of the military about it. Strong defence on the outside, strict discipline on the inside. Tommaso Campanella's City of the Sun. So many fortified naval towns like this grew up around the Baltic Sea at the time: Sveaborg, Kronstadt, all with a touch of the same pale geometry, lit by the sea. Anyone who allows himself a moment's relaxation on a fine summer's day on the terrace of the County Governor's official residence – something which is quite plausible, since Blekinge has a generous, friendly governor who believes that his fellow-citizens should have all possible access to the splendour of his own buildings, where summer concerts and poetry readings are organised in association with Blekinge Institute of Technology – cannot help but think he is by the Mediterranean. Yachts on their way in and out between the islands, the play of sunlight, a majestic hull or two on the horizon.

There are so many remarkable pages to turn in the long story of the Baltic Sea, from the barren Arctic coasts of the Gulf of Bothnia to the verdant province of Blekinge!

# *Jönköping*

The city of Jönköping is beautifully situated beside the magical blue of Lake Vättern, Sweden's second largest lake after Lake Vänern. *Vättern* quite simply means 'water'. It is deep (up to 128 metres) and long (135 kilometres) and exceptionally cold. Whenever it is covered in ice, which has only happened three times in the last fifteen years, the water clarity is immense, something that can be confirmed by both long-distance skiers and fishermen who have pitched their tents on the ice. It is warm enough for bathing in the second half of July at best, but if you feel the cold, you are well advised to wait until August.

It is extraordinary – Jönköping has been here, at the edge of Lake Vättern, for all of time. There are records of a Junaköpung as early as the 1270s. The prefix probably derives from a creek, the Junebäcken, and *köping*, of course, is an old word for a trading place. Here, in this very spot, the city has withstood the vagaries of history – and all without acknowledgment from me!

When I finally made a belated visit to this city I was confronted with something I had not expected: I instantly fell in love with it. I hope the feeling is mutual.

As you approach, in our case from the west, the town looks like a mirage beside the blue Vättern in the distance. We had to go to the hotel first, the Stora; Lars had a talk that evening in the Kristine Church, but we hadn't bothered to find out where the church or the hotel were, we just played it by ear – and our intuition led us straight to our destination without the need to consult either map or passer-by. This was obviously a sign that the town meant us well! Or perhaps one might say there is something utterly natural in the way a Swedish town has been planned and grown.

Jönköping is in what some people call the Bible Belt, an unofficial socio-geographic term that appeared towards the end of the nineteenth century – the non-conformist liberals in Jönköping and the surrounding areas wanted to distance themselves from what they saw as the more spiritually restricted congregations in the diocese of Växjö and in Kronoberg County, referring to them as if they came from 'darkest Småland'.

However, we were not heading for the non-conformists, but to the Reverend Per Arne Waldenvik, who had invited Lars together with filmmaker and writer Carl Henrik Svenstedt, to discuss the meaning of life.

So many churches in Sweden have been damaged by fire over the centuries, including this one from the seventeenth century, rebuilt after the fire and now white, unadorned and beautiful. There was a large audience of both young and old, the discussion was fruitful and the pastor proved to be an enthusiastic humanist – as the evening wore on he also proved to be an enthusiastic pipe-smoker. In the intervals a talented organist played Bach on a nineteenth-century Romantic organ and afterwards there was a little supper in the parish hall, a building originally designed by Erik Dahlberg, famous count, soldier, architect, government official and, from 1687 to 1693, County Governor in Jönköping.

It is almost always the case that the district nearest a church is one of harmony and beauty. On the walk from the church to the parish hall along the narrow pedestrian street, we discovered this to be true once again. Very few of the old houses had been pulled down and those that remained were well maintained, enhancing the peaceful atmosphere. The small square in front of the town hall was, as it said in the tourist brochure, a pearl.

Since the person writing these words spent many hours as a child in churches (in lengthy services with my own collection pennies clutched in my hand) and in parish halls (often for a sale of work by the diligent ladies of the sewing club, at which for once my little brother and I might have our own money to spend), I instantly identify with the smell and aura of these places; in contrast to many other people, and in spite of my relative lack of belief, I always feel at home in churches.

There was something particularly enjoyable about being part of a lively discussion whilst eating a delicious supper and, especially, drinking good wine in the very same parish hall, where normally a smell of coffee and home baking would predominate: something very slightly blasphemous in an agreeably exciting way for one of God's grandchildren. And our conversation was so truly uncensored that evening that the generally accepted notion of some kind of wholesome asceticism and broad intolerance in this Bible Belt was proved completely wrong. We found that the city has really been picking up over the last twenty years, with a steadily increasing population; the university, construction of new apartments overlooking the Vättern, theatre, music, restaurants and cafés all contributed to a growing prosperity.

Lake Vättern was originally a bay in the sea (we are talking of a period about 10,000 years ago) and a number of aquatic invertebrates, including the famous Vättern char, became landlocked, adapted and continue to thrive here still. This fish, with its pale pink flesh, is a true delicacy. All the restaurants around the lake with any self-respect have char on the menu. Rumour has it that the lake, which is reckoned to be bottomless, is connected to Lake Constance in the Alps. A woman who drowned in Lake Vättern is supposed to have been discovered in Lake Constance with a hymnbook from Hammar Church in her pocket ... You can choose whether you believe this story or not.

# A Hero from the Heartland of Bohuslän

A slim little yellow sign with a red border announces: Kaneröd 1. If you travel by car past Brusen in the Bullaren area, which is in southwest Sweden, near to the Norwegian border, it really feels as though you are sliding down the old gravel road. And then up again. You slip back in time as well, for in this region you are reminded that another age runs in parallel with ours; here are smallholdings still in operation, grazing animals and flowering hillsides, peace and purity in slow motion.

From this direction the forest to the right of the road looks inviting – it also slopes down steeply, then up again, and loses itself in mysterious green shadows. Each time I drive in on the narrow, winding, undulating gravel road, I feel blessed. To have so much unspoiled countryside entirely to oneself. To have the freedom to roam, anywhere at all. And then the landscape opens up again. Fields and pastures. Some roe deer are feeding over by the edge of the forest – not unduly concerned by the car, they stand perfectly still until the danger has passed.

17

A farmer sits on his small grey tractor, chugging around his land, engaged in his never-ending labour – compared with the massive red tractors on large farms, this one looks like a little toy. I see in my rear-view mirror that he is staring at my car; it is not often someone strays so far from the main roads. I feel as though I almost know him. He takes such good care of his land and is unaware of the admiration I have for him. If he realised, he would no doubt be greatly surprised.

A herd of young livestock is lying in a still-green meadow – lazily they chew the cud, twitching their ears at the flies. They have a contented air, it seems to me. I am almost shocked to see the modern world has made inroads even here – the bales of hay wrapped in plastic near the house look like teeth spewed out by a giant. And yet what I describe is not particularly remarkable – hasn't it always looked like this in the country? Yes, *has* looked. How much longer will this farmer, a hero in my eyes, care for his little farm with his animals, his tractor and his chainsaw, for his own pleasure and the delight of others who appreciate his work? Not exactly profitable, if we adopt the meaningless standards applied in agricultural politics today, is he? What will happen after he has gone?

There were more people living here in the old days. The mass emigration to America at the end of the nineteenth century caused a catastrophic drop in population in this part of the country. Be that as it may, quite a few Dutch people are moving to this part of Sweden nowadays, and Germans too, many of them living here all year round. They think Holland

18

is overcrowded and they welcome the tranquillity, calm and fresh air of this area. An example is our neighbouring farm at Tingvall, an unusually large farm for northern Bohuslän, which is run by an immigrant Dutch family. Funnily enough the newcomers say that agricultural policy is better in Sweden than in the Netherlands, though Swedish farmers complain frequently about economic conditions here, as well as the weather, of course.

Last autumn whilst on one of my mushroom-picking outings, I passed a tiny smallholding among the trees on the other side of the road. It must have been abandoned hastily for some unaccountable reason; the traditional, white, Bohuslän house is still there, its six-pane windows falling in, its roof collapsing, a young birch tree growing out through one of the windows, but still standing more or less upright. Now, however, it is far too late for anyone to save it. Thirty years ago it might have been possible. Why did no one do it then? What a waste of a house that was once so fine, in such beautiful surroundings!

In the barn of this forsaken house the remnants of human life and endeavour lie exposed: some odd, well-worn shoes, a rough scattering of dried-out hay, a wooden rake, a child's bed from long ago. An occasional garden flower valiantly pushes up between the nettles in what was once a border. On the apple tree right next to the house shrunken, sour apples – I've tasted them – are still growing. What life did the people have, who left this house to its fate? There is an almost uncanny silence. I wouldn't like to walk past here at twilight, perchance one who lived here once remains, watching over their deserted home.

I park the car as close to the ditch as I can, so there's just room on the road for another vehicle to pass. What if the farmer on the gray tractor were to appear? I want him to see that I'm considerate and mean no harm. Late summer flowers are growing at the edge of the ditch: lavender-blue scabious, yellow hawksbeard, pink and white yarrow, dainty blue bell-flowers and white sneezewort. In the vast silence of this summer's day and with a light heart I walk in through the narrow opening to one of 'my' forests. It is not entirely easy: water is running down the steep cliff that towers above the rough meadowland, gathering in a pool; rusty old barbed wire that marks the limit of long-forgotten pastures trips you up and tears at you if you're not careful. I can see it has happened to an animal before me by a tuft of coarse hair caught on the barbs.

But there, right at the edge of the field, under the sheltering branches of the enormous fir tree, are shining patches of gold. Exactly as they should be. Growing there are the huge yellow chanterelles, which look almost artificial in their perfection, a more beautiful example of *cantharellus* than in any book of mushrooms. No one apart from me appears to pick them and so it's my responsibility to make sure they are put to good use! I know that there is, that there will be, an extraordinary amount today. The basket will soon be half full. Happiness, pure and simple.

With all my senses on the alert, I carry on. There's no need to be worried about meeting a bear, as they don't venture so far south. This small farm forest has not yet been destroyed – it's still possible to roam across it easily without stumbling over tree stumps and felled branches or being vexed by the deep tracks made by outrageously large forestry machines. This is not some impenetrable spruce plantation or plundered 'regeneration site', but it does bear the mark of human beings. A collapsing stone wall has no purpose now there are no animals to graze here. How many hours of labour must have been devoted to its construction! A rusty agricultural imple-ment, half overgrown, and an unused pile of gravel attest that someone worked here. As I walk up towards the crest of the hill, making my way over the waterlogged ground, the smell of bog myrtle and stagnant water hits me. I follow one of the old tracks and am quite overwhelmed to see yellow patches of chanterelles everywhere. No one has been here! They are all mine! I just have to help myself.

I had been thinking about visiting my unknown favourite farmer for a long time and one summer it actually happened. I plucked up the courage and trudged up to the little white house, not really knowing what I was hoping for. On the door-step stood a decent pair of boots and the key was in the door! I knocked and heard someone say, 'Come in!' I took off my muddy shoes and stepped inside a small, very neat kitchen, where a tabby cat was sleeping voluptuously on the couch. An elderly man sitting at the kitchen table looked at me with a friendly expression; I told him who I was and we went on to have a delightful conversation. I asked him lots of questions about the area, the people who lived here before and who lived here now. Karl Gustaf, as the man is called, told me that since the advent of television, people didn't meet so much, whereas in the past there had always been time to sit and talk for hours, play cards or quite simply be together.

When I asked him about daring to leave his key in the lock like that, he said that people trusted each other here. He took over the farm and the forest belonging to it from his parents in the early eighties and had run it himself since then. Now he was almost eighty, and because he had macular degeneration he found it hard to see. He regretted having never married and having no children, but he told me something I found terribly romantic: every evening he took his tractor (he was not allowed to drive a car) and went to his girlfriend, who lived seven kilometres away, had dinner with her and then stayed the night. He had to leave the following morning to come back and tend the animals. He was obviously forbidden to drive because of his sight problems, but he was permitted to use his tractor. The Road Administration only wanted to know how *far* he drove. And for that he didn't use the little grey tractor, but a much more modern one.

This first meeting is the beginning of a true friendship – who would have thought it?

# *Life by a Fjord*

Sannäs Fjord in northern Bohuslän is one of only a small number of fjords in Sweden. It stretches several kilometres inland from the unspoiled fishing village of Havstenssund on the coast, past Sannäs, once also a small fishing community, with its white wooden houses and red outbuildings, and down towards the road between Tanumshede and Grebbestad. The view over the fjord is timeless – it's hard to imagine any significant changes here in the foreseeable future.

At the beginning of the 1950s my parents bought a four-hectare promontory in Sannäs Fjord, a piece of land which at that time had little value: a barren hill, a grassy hollow and a hay meadow. A few sheep grazed where the modest summer cottage now stands – because of a general construction ban, the house was actually transported to its current position on the back of a lorry, and since then it has had various extensions. Two other small cottages were moved here in the same manner – one of them was an old charcoal burner's hut, its walls seeped in black smoke. We were among the first summer visitors to this district and it was our great pleasure to spend time with the fishermen, farmers and other permanent residents.

The houses are not worth much, but the piece of land has increased in value. I wonder what Oskar Niklasson, the man who sold it to my parents for 8,000 kronor, would have thought if he'd known his meagre plot would be worth several million today. He had a smallholding, did a little subsistence fishing and was employed as the verger in the Havstenssund church, to which he cycled in all weathers. He lived, alone, in straitened circumstances.

Some farming still goes on in the area, but there are mostly equestrian centres and horses where once there were fields of cows. The biggest change to the land is the proliferation of newly constructed holiday homes, and the proprietors all have large fast boats that survive the onslaught of winter ice at their shared moorings on the jetty.

I remember a clear fjord, teeming with fish; we laid nets, something permitted in those days, and always had a motley catch, including plaice. In our water there was also an oyster bed, for which we had a licence, and if we had unexpected guests at the house all we had to do was run down to the shore and gather fresh mussels at a depth of no more than half a metre, right by the edge. Every summer a school of porpoises would come in search of fish and we would all rush out of the house to watch in awe. We would troll for mackerel too; sometimes we had a massive catch and Mum would bake them in butter with breadcrumbs and dill – heavenly. Just some of the sea creatures living in the fjord in the fifties were: dab, flounder, plaice, cod, whiting, mackerel, herring, porpoise, salmon, trout, eel, sculpin, prawn, crab, lobster, oyster and mussel. And for us this was all perfectly natural. Environmental destruction was unheard of in those days.

In the crevices on the rocky hillside we picked kilos of sweet raspberries that Dad made into jam. And the little wooded areas in the gullies between the cliffs were overflowing with chanterelles and other mushrooms. Was it seventh heaven?

It really *was* a kind of paradise – what more could anyone wish for? Sitting here now, more than fifty years later, directly opposite the island of Killingen and the conservation area that will never be developed, looking at the abiding beauty of the view, listening to the screech of the gulls and breathing in the distinctive smells of the fjord, I am filled with melancholy and deep concern. The condition of the fjord has deteriorated. There are almost no circles to be seen on the surface from fish darting beneath, the water by the shore is distinctly murky, the bottom is much muddier than before, there are far fewer seabirds and, at the moment, while it's calm, clumps of algae are floating in a green sludge at the water's edge and trailing seaweed wraps around your legs if you try to bathe. A few pleasure boats pass by at full speed. Why are they always in such a hurry? Surely here it should be all about the journey and not the destination? The sunset is just as breathtakingly beautiful and red as it ever was; and the fading light cloaks both land and water in a magical haze as evening becomes night.

For years a laundry was allowed to release phosphates into the fjord – we didn't understand then how dangerous it was. The poisonous anti-fouling paint on boats, boat fuel, discharge from agriculture and motor vehicles, household sewage, overfishing, acid rain – it has all contributed to our destruction of the marine environment. The downside of what we call progress and prosperity. But the people living by the fjord for a few weeks every summer don't know what it once was like. No doubt they think everything is as it should be, because they have never known anything else. Their time is now and they proceed on that basis.

Thousands of tourists and second-home owners come to enjoy the unique surroundings of Tanum Municipality in the summer season, for the bathing, the boating and the sun. There are around twelve thousand permanent residents, a number that increases fourfold in summer. The pollution in Sannäs Fjord and other marine environments is not the fault of the relatively poor west coast communities. Several projects are under way to improve the situation in and around Sannäs Fjord: sediment and organisms on the seabed are being analysed, old outlets recorded, marshland created, damaging agricultural discharges monitored, applications made for EU funding, and more.

But one single municipality cannot do a great deal about global problems. Politicians and others in positions of responsibility say that we can't turn back the clock – as if some sort of nostalgia is behind the irony in the expression 'it was better before'.

No, in this place unmistakeable, essential values have been lost. Forever?

# *Wolves*

If you utter the word 'wolf' you will instantly be embroiled in a lively exchange and one that rapidly assumes a more aggressive tone. It's similar to broaching religious matters at an alcohol-imbued party. It excites passions you never expected. For Swedes can be divided into two distinct camps: those who want to conserve the wolf population as part of Sweden's fauna, and those who want to get rid of it. Very few people are indifferent to the fate of the wolf. Like the bear, the lynx and the devil, the wolf belongs to a group of creatures that no one in old peasant society dared even to name, for fear of summoning up the dreaded being. One of many euphemisms or innocuous nicknames for the devil is The Evil One, a bear is a teddy, a lynx was called a *gaupa* and a wolf might be called Old Grey Legs, among other things.

The wolf became a protected species in Sweden in 1966, but some culling has been permitted for livestock owners, when their domestic animals are subject to attack. In 2011 the Swedish Environmental Protection Agency issued licences to hunt wolves; the intention was to strengthen the gene pool of the inbred stock by shooting some and replacing them with new wolves introduced from countries such as Russia. With a quota of twenty wolves, 7,400 hunters registered – a case of the many against one. In 2012 the hunt was banned after criticism from the EU that the Swedish wolf hunt was jeopardising the survival of Sweden's wolf population. Sweden has a long border with its neighbour, Norway, and when a count was made in both countries between 2010 and 2011 a combined total of 289 to 325 wolves was estimated, the majority of them in Sweden. Wolves are no respecters of borders, and besides, we dispensed with passport requirements long ago between our historically connected countries.

Selma Lagerlöf wrote about Gösta Berling and his beloved Anna Stjärnhök travelling in a sleigh through a sparkling, snowy winter's night in Värmland, pursued by a terrifying pack of wolves. The lovers narrowly escaped death; Gösta had to beat off the wolves with his whip as they reached the very steps to the house. At another point in Gösta Berling's saga she describes the wilds of Värmland: 'That's where the wolves live; they come out at night and chase the peasant's sleigh, until the mother has to take the little child sitting on her knee and throw it out to them, to save her own life and her husband's.'

Perhaps she helped foster Swedes' ingrained fear or, if anything, abhorrence of wolves. The wolf has always been a symbol of malevolence, even if for some people, the zookeepers at Skansen for instance, it as an exceptionally inquisitive and social animal. If you are ever allowed into the enclosure there with one of the handlers you'll see that a wolf will come up to you almost like a dog and let you pat it. You might even get a lick on the cheek ... But so many stories, such as 'Little Red Riding Hood' and, much earlier, Aesop's Fables, depict the wolf in an intimidating, or at the very least, unsympathetic way.

A marked fear of wolves still exists in urban Sweden, despite only one known instance of a wolf killing people that dates back to 1821. In this case a wolf had been captured as a cub and had grown up among humans before eventually being released; after so much time it had lost its instinct for hunting food and so it came back to the village where it had lived, and killed young children.

Wolves often destroy large numbers of sheep or other farm animals without consuming all the flesh, making the expression 'as hungry as a wolf' quite enlightening. Animals lost in this way are indemnified by the state (though some may prove to have been killed by dogs) but the anger and sorrow felt by their owners is thoroughly understandable. It's awful too when wolves attack and kill dogs that have been allowed loose during a walk in the forest; wolves obviously see the dogs as rivals on their territory.

Close to our house in rural Bohuslän, on the opposite side of the lake, there is a large wilderness area called Kynnefjäll. The Swedish word *fjäll* normally means 'mountain', but in this case the closest meaning is the English word 'highland'. On Kynnefjäll there are forests, swamps, moors, lakes, there's a

29

multitude of wild animals, especially elk, foxes and deer, and even wolves, lynx and beavers, but there's a scarcity of human beings.

Last summer two women, summer residents out picking mushrooms and calmly minding their own business, had an alarming experience – they had discovered a wonderful chanterelle patch and were delightedly filling their baskets, when they heard a howl. Soon afterwards they heard a howl from another direction, and then another, and another. Seized by pure panic, the women abandoned their baskets and, with powers they didn't know they possessed, climbed up into a tree. They couldn't *see* the wolves, but they could *hear* them. Their mobile phones didn't work out there in the wilds, but they were able to ring the emergency number 112. They were rescued eventually, taking their mushrooms home with them (wolves don't like mushrooms), and despite their adventure these two valiant women afterwards declared their strong support for keeping wolves in Sweden.

Wolf experts thought that the howling was from a family of wolves whose members had dispersed in various directions to hunt and were now calling one another back together in the afternoon. And the rest of us were urged by the experts not to be deterred by the presence of wolves in the area, but to carry on picking our mushrooms and our berries. I for one would love to meet a wolf when I'm out in the forest. But a chance meeting with a bear, on the other hand, would give me a seizure – I'm sure I'd die of fright before the bear had

30

a chance to do me in. Normally both bears and wolves avoid human beings – and who can blame them?

Today the wolf is regarded as an endangered species in Sweden. But what about biodiversity – don't wolves contribute to that too?

# First Signs of Spring

'It was not night, nor was it day, it hovered in between them' writes the Swedish poet Elias Tegnér in his epic Viking poem *Frithiof's Saga* in 1825. Now, at the beginning of April, 2011, these words can be used to describe the weather in Sweden in early spring: It was not winter, nor was it spring, it hovered in between them. So true, but of course the rhythm of Tegnér's original is lost. When the weather chart is showing spring, sun and gentle breezes down on the continent of Europe, winter hangs on stubbornly up here. And it lasts a long time. The last two winters have been almost as cold and snowy as the war winters of the forties.

April is a capricious month in Sweden; the weather alternates between hours of sunshine, when Swedes can turn their faces up to the sun in an attitude of thanksgiving, and heavy snowfall, when they screw up their faces, hunch their shoulders and lean forward to shelter themselves from its cursed, icy forces.

March has been grey and bleak and everyone has looked forward with dogged perseverance to a change. I have a few days left in which to prepare my all-too-large garden before the arrival of spring. Colours are muted, the pale yellow-green of the lawn contrasts with the light brown of the autumn leaves swirling in the gusts of wind. The branches on the birch tree are a brownish purple colour that will soon turn to light green when the buds start to burst. Dainty white snowdrops quiver in the wind amidst the leaves in the borders. The last of the snow has all but disappeared after the spring rain, except for some shaded north-facing spots where it still lies in small, dirty patches.

Today, 9 April, the disintegrating ice has disappeared as if by magic and the water set free. Already the waves are rising higher in the fresh breeze. From the immense, rolling fields on the horizon the loud bugle call of the cranes can be heard. They gather here at this time of year, standing in small groups on their alarmingly long, thin legs, before the start of the breeding season.

It must be the same pair of great tits that have found their way back to their old home in a small pipe protruding from the veranda only half a metre above the flowerbed. Is it really a sensible choice of abode? Aren't they afraid of the cat? Surely parents and babies must be disturbed by us tramping above their roof? There are so many bird sounds to be heard – and as usual I'm annoyed that I recognise so few of them. It's too late now to improve my knowledge. But loudest of all are the cranes in the distant fields.

On a windy day like this it's not worth raking up the piles of leaves that fell last October and November from the tall maple trees and oaks next to the house. Besides, it's a horribly boring job, carting load after load to the compost heap, and I'm happy to postpone it for a while. But I know it has to be done – under the layer of leaves there are hidden bulbs, desperate to be uncovered so they can reach the light. At night the temperature nears zero again. Our poor old country!

But the following day the world is a different place. Early in the morning the sun is already shining and warm in the still air. Spring has arrived overnight. A frisky bee is buzzing around the snowdrops and look! – an early Brimstone butterfly, a gorgeous yellow, flutters past. I sit in a sunny corner with my coffee and my paper and delight in the beauty around me. It's not strange that weather is one of the most common topics of conversation in Sweden. In the tropics, where the sun shines all the time, the subject is no doubt less impelling.

The flowerbeds are liberated from last year's leaves and after only a few hours yellow, white and purple crocuses are bursting out. Only someone who has been huddled up, sniffling and shivering, through a long winter can truly understand the euphoria of spring. And even if we know in Sweden that there *can* be setbacks – snow might fall on the first of May – we give free rein to our spring fever.

Twenty kilometres to the west is the Skagerrak. Despite all that needs doing in the garden at the moment, we can't resist making a visit to the nature reserve in the area called Tjurpannan, which lies to the southwest of Havstenssund. Conscious that we are the first to tread here this year, stepping on virgin land, we say very little to each other, silenced by the breathtaking landscape around us and filled with a sense of spirituality.

In Tjurpannan there is no outer archipelago offering protection – seafarers were right to be afraid of the treacherous rocks and reefs and the stormy water's unbridled rage, when it pounds against the cliffs in a deafening onslaught and flings its spume high into the air. Many sailors have drowned here, and there is even a story about the infamous souls in this wretched part of Bohuslän who lit fires on the beaches, thus duping the poor men in their boats who had been caught out by the ferocity of the weather and were desperately trying to reach land, where they would soon be robbed and murdered by those ashore.

We follow a little track over bare ground and rocks, where plants such as creeping juniper, hawthorn, honeysuckle and dog rose are shaped by the storms. There are no tall trees to be seen here; everything is bent by the elements and grows close to the ground.

An early adder, still rather lethargic, slithers across the path in front of us. Huge fields of shingle, protected nowadays, are a reminder of how this land was formed long ago. What amazing forces must have been at work then! In the cliffs there are potholes and bands of basalt in the granite, known as 'Satan's Harrow', as if the devil himself has ploughed the cliff. The character of the landscape is ancient and primeval – on the heath a little way off there is some water-starwort and the grass is still pale and tangled. An area right by the sea is fenced off and later in the year there will be animals grazing there, keeping the vegetation down, the very same types of animal that would have been found in an early agricultural settlement. There is not really a great deal for them to eat.

The sun is shining and it warms the air slightly, but the wind is chilly and the sea before us is bluer than blue – we can see that a solitary sailor has ventured out already. The rocks at the edge look gently rounded, rinsed clean, and almost smooth. But it would be suicidal to set foot on them just now: one wrong step on the slippery rock and you would fall into the surging swell. And if you were not knocked unconscious against the rocks, it would still be impossible to haul yourself out, with nothing to grab hold of.

But in summer they are delightfully comfortable to lie on, your body moulding itself to their shape. When we were here one day last August, we could detect a disgusting smell from a long way off, and as we approached we could see some kind of marine mammal, several metres long, washed up among the stones on the beach. There is no trace of it now.

Most of the coastal flowers are in bud, but have not yet started to bloom. By the sea the climate is harsher than inland and everything is later. Soon there will be thrift, wild pansies, dog roses, bog bilberries, sea-kale and other littoral plants.

Often we are completely alone on our rambles, but on this day of wonderful summery weather we meet small groups of other nature lovers and, in this region so close to the border, we hear many of them speaking Norwegian.

# Smile of a Midsummer Night

The grass is swaying gently in the June breeze. A period of rain has just come to an end and it looks as though Midsummer's Eve will be as glorious as we've been hoping all year. 'A June night never happens, it's more like a dew-pearled day', the poet Harry Martinson wrote. A night when dusk slips into dawn. Above the Arctic Circle, where the sun doesn't set, it stays light all night long: the magical land of the midnight sun. For many people it seems a waste to go to bed at all on a night when nature is almost too exquisite; how can a mere earthly being measure up to all this beauty? And all you want on Midsummer's Eve is to have someone with whom you can share your feelings. 'One should not sleep, one should be two ...'

In common with a number of other Swedish festivals, mid-summer has pre-Christian, pagan roots. Nature held a special significance in times when supernatural forces were at play. A primitive sacrifice to the gods of fertility may be the origin of our midsummer celebration; it was associated with the longest day, what we call the summer solstice, an event our heathen forbears were able to forecast. Nowadays Midsummer's Eve is always a Friday between 19 and 25 June.

The unique traditions essential to midsummer celebrations are actually no more than a century old. Let's begin with the food and the decision on what we should serve this year. We'll be sitting outside to eat, of course, unless it's absolutely pouring, even if the evening might be cool. But as Wikipedia drily states: 'There is a strong drinking tradition associated with midsummer celebrations, making it one of the weekends in the year when most drunken disorderliness occurs'.

And that's the way it is. Naturally beer and aquavit accompany the food, and if you've primed yourself with aquavit, you hardly feel the cold. To go with the drink it's essential to have new potatoes – if the worst comes to the worst and the Swedish crop isn't ready, we import potatoes from somewhere warmer – and different types of herring with sour cream and chives, the quintessential taste of midsummer, with crisp bread, butter and assorted cheeses. The contents of the main course can vary – it's not as crucial as the herring and new potato – but we *have* to get hold of Swedish strawberries for dessert, whatever the cost, which can be quite considerable.

Before the meal we dance round the maypole with our children and friends, a custom we borrowed from Germany at the end of the Middle Ages. On our heads are beautiful wreaths of flowers that, by rights, we should have made ourselves – our forefathers believed they could capture the forces of summer in a garland, in preparedness for the rest of the year. We hold each other by the hand and dance in large circles round the tall pole, with its cross at the top and covered in birch twigs and decorated with Swedish flags and an array of midsummer wild flowers: daisies, clover, chamomile, forget-me-nots, harebells, yarrow, columbine and many others. Traditionally two garlands hang from the short cross beam, but there are many local variations of the maypole. Raising the pole is something of a challenge, but we manage it, with a little teamwork.

There are so many songs to be sung and danced to, games to be played, fun and frolics to be enjoyed. In the old days fights were not uncommon in rural communities – aquavit can be at the root of many a mischief. If we're lucky we'll have a group of musicians in our midst, perhaps with traditional instruments such as the accordion, fiddle or *nyckelharpa*. If you have never seen Swedes dancing round the maypole, you might be rather surprised to witness grown men and women dancing to 'Little Frogs', the highlight of which has everyone squatting down and hopping clumsily round the pole (and wrecking their backs!), pretending to be frogs, using their hands to illustrate the ears and tails frogs lack:

Little frogs
Little frogs
Are funny to observe.
No tails
No tails
No ears do they possess.

But it's all for the children, as we say.

According to tradition, before retiring to bed you should go out into the fields to pick seven (or sometimes nine) different kinds of flowers to place under your pillow. After you've gathered your posy, you shouldn't speak, and then you'll have a dream about your future spouse, a dream that will come true. Some people say you have to jump over seven roundpole fences too, but finding those nowadays is no mean feat.

Midsummer and regret go hand in hand. It's not just the drinking that makes us so melancholy on this particular evening, not to mention the following Midsummer's Day. All the dreams and all the hopes, so seldom fulfilled, are slightly overwhelming. The wonderful Swedish summer lies ahead of us, of course, but the year has reached its turning point and from now on the nights are slowly drawing in.

And the grass is swaying in the June breeze.

# The Vanished East of Sweden

Sometimes visitors come from distant places, maybe Texas, or China, here, to the home of writers and artists, Södermalm in Stockholm. They are captivated by the beauty they see around them from the number two bus route and the view from Stigbergsgatan, and impressed by the colossal size of the Baltic ferries. A very common question on their lips is: how did Sweden's capital end up in such a strange place, on the easternmost edge of the country, by a sea which has no direct links with any continent other than its own? Why not Gothenburg? From there surely you have access to all the oceans in the world? Or why not Östersund, so close to the centre of the country, and by a beautiful lake?

The answer is simple for those of us who know. Stockholm *is* in the centre – of an old kingdom that no longer exists.

On a globe you can locate the centre wherever you want. In the Byzantine Empire the centre of the world was the place in the Hagia Sophia in Constantinople where emperors were crowned. The Lord High Chancellor of Sweden, Axel Oxenstierna, had another idea. In 1640, during the reign of Queen

Christina, he drew up a plan for Sweden to have two capitals and for the regent to alternate between two royal residences: Stockholm and Narva. According to the plan, Stockholm on its own was far too westerly for the needs of the square-shaped Swedish kingdom. Narva, close to where the Narva River flows into the southern Gulf of Finland – a pile of rubble after the German retreat from Estonia and a wretched place during the immense brutality of Soviet imperial dominion with the displacement of population and mass murder it brought – is still today a border town between real Europe and vast, unfathomable Russia. In 1640 Narva was a flourishing town with great potential for expansion and an ideal centre for Sweden's almost colonial development of Livland and Ingermanland. For centuries Narva remained the outer limit of western civilisation, rather in the style of the *Lord of the Rings* – a grim, austere frontier stronghold against the land of Mordor and its dark fortresses on the other side of the river, or like two opposing rooks on the chessboard.

We have the benefit of hindsight. We know, or think we know, something – not all – about the appalling suffering of the Baltic countries, first under German occupation and then for decades under the Soviet Union. We know that Finland would have endured exactly the same fate, if the young republic had not managed to unite in 1939 and inflict on the Red Army one of the greatest defeats in world history: a Thermopylae that every living Swede today should be grateful for.

What is remarkable is the strange repression, almost in the

psychoanalytical sense, which has for so long characterised public discussion in Sweden of the Baltic question, and perhaps especially the lives and destinies of Swedes in the Baltic area. This is not just an allusion to the unbelievable statement by the former Minister of Foreign Affairs, Sten Andersson, that Estonia, Latvia and Lithuania were not subject to Soviet occupation. What in God's name were they then? It refers to an extensive culture of which Swedish Finland is almost the only part remaining, with the idyllic villages and lovely summer cottages of Åboland as a kind of ideal. Of course, Tomas Tranströmer wrote the long poem *Baltics*, not without significance despite being poetry. Carl Bildt, Per Unckel and many others were staunch supporters of the regular Monday meetings on Norrmalmstorg.

But my own impression over the years has been of a perverse boycott of any discussion of the Baltic countries, the reasons for which are extremely complex, and influenced not just by the imported propaganda machine of the Soviet bloc, but also by a subtle feeling of guilt.

Who today knows that in 1900 Saint Petersburg had as many Swedish inhabitants as turn-of-the-century Västerås? Among them was the Nobel family, for example, and the parents of poet Edith Södergran, members of an entire intellectual and industrial elite. Or that in the place where Saint Petersburg now stands there was once a Swedish stronghold on the banks of the Neva River?

Present-day Sweden's back is turned to the East. And is likely to remain so.

# *Journey on a Number Two Bus*

The large, matronly number two bus goes from Barnängen in Södermalm as far as Norrtull in Norrmalm, thus travelling diagonally across almost the whole of the Stockholm's inner city. The number two is one of the more reliable buses – it's frequent, sometimes even arrives early, and its route is one of the most beautiful. I sometimes wonder if its drivers might not also be a little jollier and friendlier than those on other buses.

Early in the morning from our window, which is close to the number two terminus at Barnängen Manor, we can see a crowd of people, dressed in black, waiting in the penetrating cold of this February day, every one of them wrapped in his or her own silence, on their way to work.

When it gets a little lighter it's time for the nursery children; mums and dads with little children pack onto the buses, many racing up, pushing buggies in front of them, as if it's the finish of a hundred-metre sprint, all of them having arrived at the same time on the ferry from the new housing development in Hammarby Sjöstad. The town planners had intended this part of town to be for elderly people who wanted to sell up and downsize, offering them considerable comfort and at the same time the luxury of being able to have their own boat right outside on Hammarby Lake; instead the area has been populated largely by young parents and children. Something of a planning fiasco. Nurseries and schools had to be built in haste for the new inhabitants. The infants, contained within their own little subculture, peer at one another with interest, once they're safely installed on the bus and their parents have started tapping on their iPhones – a girl stops sobbing the instant she catches the eye of a little fellow prisoner in the buggy next to hers. Occasionally a parent will be sidetracked and smile intensely at a favoured child.

We retired from paid employment some time ago and if we have errands to run in town we don't usually go for the bus before ten or eleven o'clock, when there are fewer people around. You see one or two elderly gentlemen with their rollator walking aids, white-haired old ladies chatting with their friends as they have done their whole lives, and young people as well, engrossed in mobile phone conversations from which fascinating snippets can be heard. A little army of nursery children wearing colourful clothes and miniature backpacks marches up to the bus stop, two by two, hand in hand, under the firm guidance of the assistants, probably on their way to the nearby toy museum or tram museum; they board the bus and soon after alight in just as orderly a fashion, unlike the rowdy gang of middle school students from Sofia School, also on their way somewhere. We witness a phenomenon we remember well from similar trips at their age: the leaders of the pack charge to the back of the bus and occupy the most desirable seats – while the poor teacher does her best to keep the braying mob together. When everyone has finally settled down, the quietness and relief is palpable. The rest of us breathe out and collectively spare a sympathetic, and very grateful, thought for the teacher.

The bus follows its famed route high above the water along Katarinavägen down to Slussen. The view over Saltsjön with the silhouette of the magnificent historic buildings and church spires of Stockholm's city centre in the background is one of the most beautiful of any urban environment – a complimentary extra for the bus travellers who are being conveyed, some more willingly than others, to work or school or elsewhere.

It has been immortalised in world literature by August Strindberg; in 'A Bird's Eye View of Stockholm', the first chapter in his novel about Stockholm society, *The Red Room* (1879), he describes how the wind comes in from the sea far away in the distance, past Sjötullen, over the water along Sicklaön, towards Danviken, where the wind 'takes fright' (because of the insane inmates of Danviken mental hospital) and rushes on to Stadsgården wharf far below us, which in his day would have reeked of coal, tar and fish oil, but today smells mostly of exhaust fumes from all the vehicles, and then up and on to the little garden in Mosebacke.

A huge Baltic ferry, more like a floating pleasure palace than a boat, is moored at the quay below us, distorting the perspective and obscuring some of the beauty. But the superb view is still substantially the same as the one Strindberg saw at the end of the nineteenth century, and the screeching of the gulls sounds the same today as it did then.

At Slussen the bus almost empties and the people run frantically, often flouting red lights, towards the underground and their onward journey. Slussen is an important and popular place at the junction between the districts of Södermalm and Gamla Stan, but it's also a series of locks connecting Lake Mälaren with Saltsjön – the site is known too for the ingenious design of the cloverleaf roundabout, built in 1935. Katarinahissen, a public passenger lift opened in 1936, rises above it all and links Katarinavägen with Mosebacke Torg, where Strindberg's novel begins. Under the footbridge between the lift and Mosebacke is the Gondolen Restaurant, formed like a futuristic airship gondola in the style of the 1930s, one of Stockholm's restaurant classics, where you can enjoy an excellent meal while looking out over the water and the city with a truly Strindbergian bird's eye view.

The whole of the area around Slussen is now under the threat of radical redevelopment, provoking a highly sceptical response from Stockholmers.

But the bus trundles on; it passes Skeppsbron and the vast Royal Palace and sweeps round Kungsträdgården, 'King's Park', enshrined forever in the history of the modern city as a result of the Battle for the Elms, over trees which were going to be felled to make way for a new underground station, but were saved by a massive public protest. Yes, look! They're still standing!

The traveller on the bus can also catch a glimpse of the white boats at the quay below the Nobel Prize winners' hotel, the Grand, moored there until they head out into the archipelago with their passengers. On this particular day they are accompanied by hundreds of white swans, who have obviously chosen this venue for a meeting. Food is provided on the giant bird table alongside.

The bus continues, stopping at Norrmalmstorg where a group of well-dressed, immaculately coiffured gentlemen board, presumably on their way to an important meeting or a business lunch, and anticipation rises as the bus approaches Stureplan, the hub on Friday and Saturday evenings of the city's nightlife and exclusive bars and clubs.

Here the major streets of Kungsgatan, Birger Jarlsgatan, Biblioteksgatan and Sturegatan converge and the square is always bustling. At the warmest times of the year you feel as though you are somewhere more continental than Stockholm; it is packed with restaurants, bars and outside cafés, but the beautiful people flock around the Sturehof, which was established as a bar in 1897 and has maintained its dominance as a watering hole rich in tradition ever since.

A strange phenomenon in Stockholm on Friday and Saturday evenings is the queuing; people are prepared to stand in line outside bars, keeping on the right side of some muscular bouncer who's monitoring the whole affair. Only those of the highest status are able to jump the queue for some of the bars around Stureplan. You know you are Someone when you sail into the warmth under the jealous or impressed gaze of the rest of the queue.

But all this is of no consequence to the bus, which continues along Birger Jarlsgatan and turns into Odengatan, past Gunnar Asplund's famous public library with its characteristic central cylinder, another building in danger of unsympathetic expansion, although halted for the time being.

After chugging up towards Odenplan the bus finally reaches Norrtull, its destination, where two old toll houses from the eighteenth century escaped the demolition craze of the 1960s and are still standing. It really feels as though the true stone city, the city within the tolls, ends here. And at the busy traffic intersection we enter a completely separate district, Solna.

# Sounds of the City

One single man has been all men, Borges wrote in his wonderful prose poem about William Shakespeare.

It's tempting to echo this: one single Stockholmer has been all Stockholmers. And that is August Strindberg.

Strindberg returned home after one of his long visits abroad at the end of the 1890s and found everything to be different. The changes were perhaps not as great as those between the 1950s and the second millennium encountered by a returning expatriate today, but Strindberg knew nothing of that.

Whereas writers of the 1960s and 1970s experienced the grotesque demolition of the central district around Malmskillnadsgatan and the soulless brutalism and desolation of the newly created Sergels Torg as something thoroughly negative, Strindberg's reactions to the sweeping changes of his time were entirely positive.

Gone were the old tobacco fields and the small wooden houses that could now only be found in one or two isolated parts of Södermalm. Instead the attributes of a modern city were visible: avenues and boulevards like Paris and Berlin; tall, grandiose facades harbouring dark apartments in courtyards at the back for the servants and the less well-to-do.

The word 'modern' appears in Strindberg's intricate stage directions for at least two of his five chamber plays.

> The facade of a modern house with basement of granite, the upper part of brick and yellow stucco; the window casements and ornaments of sandstone; in the middle of the basement a low portal to the courtyard …

The 'modern' element is important.

Also fascinating are the sound effects the dramatist Strindberg introduces into the various stage directions. When the curtain rises in *The Storm* the ringing of many different church bells can be heard. In *The Ghost Sonata* the sound effects read as follows:

> A steamboat's bell is heard, and now and then the base notes from the organ in a nearby church penetrate the silence.

For someone living in Södermalm in the 2010s these little audio vignettes, made long before modern recording techniques – the only one of Strindberg is a rasping phonograph cylinder – have special curiosity value.

It's possible that many different church bells can still be heard ringing through the crisp, frosty air on a New Year's Eve.

But on a normal day it's hard to hear the bells above the noise of the traffic. The biggest difference between the Stockholm of Strindberg's chamber plays and today's city is undoubtedly the shrill whine of the trains as they pass over the high bridges, the drone of jet aircraft flying in over Hammarby Lake bound for the airport at Bromma and the ever-present hum of motor vehicles. No horses and carriages. No regimental trumpets. On the rare occasion when a princess is wed or a foreign head of state makes an official visit, there is the dull thud of a 21-gun salute on Skeppsholmen. Strindberg had a fascination for military signals, from the reveille to the last post, and his interpretation of the sounds of a military tattoo could be humorous, as in this example from his 1882 book, *Gamla Stockholm*:

> *The Lifeguard is going to join God*
> the trumpets sound ...
> *If he's lucky, if he's lucky*
> the drums reply.

The modern city strikes up with a great deal more volume and monotone. Underground trains decelerate and accelerate in glissando, ambulances wail like wolves on a winter's night in Västerbotten. From Vitabergsparken on a summer evening the wind can carry the repetitive thumping of an outdoor party, one rock singer indistinguishable from the next. In the city centre hotel guests are disturbed by painful low-frequency throbbing from nightclub loudspeakers. This Stockholm has been transformed by combustion engines and electronics to another acoustic world. Perhaps the background noise that Strindberg conceived as a dramatic enhancement of the visual set would appear tame, obscure and innocuous today?

Yet one sound that has remained constant is of children playing in the courtyard on an evening in September, balls rolling across the grass, high-spirited squeals and indignant shouts, signs of a children's world that has been here all the time. Even as long ago as the nineteenth century. And even longer than that.

Only we are the ones who perpetually leave it behind.

# What do Swedes do?

Every Sunday when I walk into my old newsagent's to buy a paper, a whole new world opens up. As soon as I open the door I can feel the crowded, yet animated atmosphere. There are rarely more than a couple of customers in there at the same time. But today! A Sunday! The shop is transformed into a casino. The patrons look neither sophisticated nor gangster types – forget all those films you've seen of gamblers as beautiful, glamorous people in evening dress, slender cigarette holder in one hand and glass in the other. Forget the youngsters too, standing in front of a row of one-armed bandits that they jerk and wrench until, with any luck, a heap of jingling coins is spewed out.

No, these are people of a certain age, most of them so-called 'grey panthers'. In the slushy snow outside the shop there is both a rollator and a kicksled, not a chauffeur-driven limousine in sight. The shop walls are covered with congratulatory announcements of winnings, in one or two cases of up to 100,000 kronor. Folk stand in a long queue as they wait their turn, joking about good luck and bad luck, and they hand in their coupons with optimism gleaming in their eyes. Many of them are hoping for a win to supplement their meagre pension or enhance their salary. They also crave a little excitement. Maybe they'll win next time. The chance that this shop, which once sold a big winning ticket and 'has luck on its side', can produce more big wins than other shops is statistically against all the odds. 'Dice have no memory', a mathematician would say.

Outside the shop the church bells are calling the faithful to worship – a brief investigation reveals that there are only eighteen of them at the service today in the church a stone's throw from the square – it's obviously something a Swede does less and less. He seems to have closed his ears to the church's promise that he will receive his reward in heaven, opting instead for the instant possibility of a reward here on earth. Around seventy-two per cent of the population are still members of the Church of Sweden, formerly the state church. The number has reduced by ten per cent in ten years – the same applies to the evangelical free churches.

Otherwise, Swedes spend a lot of time on the sofa in front of the television. At the end of the week families delight in 'Cosy Friday', buying in sweets, crisps and soft drinks – something stronger for the adults of course. They gather round a hired film or watch television. To avoid family arguments it's not unusual to have more than one set in a household. For a number of years the press has formed an unholy alliance with television – as seen in the massive newspaper headlines the day after the most popular programmes have been aired.

A clear case of cross-fertilisation. After a programme such as 'Let's Dance', for example, the contestants' answers, outfits, appearance and shortcomings are all the subject of animated comment and analysis, be it in the form of newspaper billboards, articles in the paper or posts on the internet – and viewers' comments are brimming with excited indignation. A soap star might be in the headlines for years, but will soon be forgotten. Interest is high in whoever is going out in 'Farmer Wants a Wife' or 'Single Mums' and whoever is still in with a chance to date, or even marry, the farmer or the mum – but it's fleeting.

Swedes can be quite family orientated – there's a baby boom even in the cities. A Swedish woman will give birth to 1.86 children, a good figure by European standards. Social support for childbearing and childcare is better here than in most other European countries. At popular cafés in Stockholm there are always scores of buggies, a feature which actually annoys some people but which should really be acknowledged for the excellent thing it is. Who else is going to look after so many of us, the baby boomers of the forties, when we eventually require care? A hostile debate has also raged over whether it is acceptable for mothers to breastfeed their babies in public. Those who are against have obviously suppressed any thought of how they themselves received their nourishment when they were small.

Does a Swede have time to read books, people wonder anxiously, especially those who moan about degenerate youth and reckon everything was better before. Opinions on this are divided: according to the central statistical office, Statistics Sweden, reading has decreased marginally since 1980 (it is difficult to formulate questions that will adequately elicit sensible responses), but according to Eurostat, a directorate-general of the European Commission, Sweden emerged top in a recent poll which asked the following question of Europeans in their different countries: 'How many times in the last year have you read a book?' What a Swede reads remains unanswered. Swedish authors would seem to be mainly writing crime novels, the more unrealistic, brutal and gory the better. And, as is well known, these crime novels are extremely popular abroad. Exactly how do these books affect Sweden's image, I wonder?

Despite the average Swede being engaged in a perpetual battle to lose weight, seventy-four food programmes are shown on Swedish television channels in a normal week – according to a report in the evening paper *Expressen*, and therefore undeniably true. The purchase of kitchen gadgets and the sale of cookbooks have reached record levels – even though less time than ever is being devoted to food preparation. The skilled housewife, whose kitchen was her territory, is no more. Glossy photographs in recipe books serve as some kind of pornography for us to sit and drool over. On television it's predominantly male chefs who prepare the food and it's all about the 'art of cooking'. But the audience is mainly female and it's still women shouldering the double burden, cooking in the kitchen at home and clearing up after a man who has produced his culinary masterpiece. As one television critic expressed it: 'Swedish women renounce generations of silent toil in their own kitchens, to watch self-important men shouting and screaming in TV kitchens.'

So how do Swedes live? Very well, thank you, is the answer to that. There's plenty of space. But our homes are swallowing up an ever greater proportion of our hard-earned cash. For some strange reason buying your own flat in Stockholm is much more expensive than in any other Nordic city. And property-owning is increasing to the detriment of the rental sector. In Stockholm city centre the affluent middle classes have almost totally taken over. Everyone else is pushed further out. Young people setting their foot on the first rung of the property ladder are facing outrageously high mortgages.

And of course we have our summer cottage culture. The Swedish dream is of a little red cottage by a lake, to potter around in the garden and get close to nature – only a few generations ago most people lived in the country. Far more than fifty per cent of Swedes have access to a second home and according to statistics there are 558,455 second homes (they're not called summer cottages any more) in Sweden. So the average Swede has two homes. Many rural properties are silent, locked up and abandoned during the winter months, but filled with life at weekends in spring and all through the delightful summer, short though it might be, when we have to stock up on as much sun and fresh air as possible to make it through the long dark winter.

Camping is also growing in popularity with record numbers staying in Swedish campsites: last summer there were more than fifteen million overnight stays, and more and more European visitors are drawn here when sites in their own countries are overbooked. That little green scout tent you remember from childhood is completely obsolete – now it's a question of a huge campervan at the very least.

But Swedes need to get out into the countryside – at any price! If you want to make one general point about 'a typical Swede' (here you will definitely find yourself on shaky ground), you can with justification declare that the tie between a Swede and nature is very strong. We take the Right of Public Access as a given; we are at liberty to walk wherever we like without any regard for the landowner. As a matter of fact, it's amazing how seldom one meets any other human being when roaming about in the forests and fields!

# *My Childhood Nockebytorg*

The old number twelve tram still rattles along between Nockeby and Alvik, but it doesn't rattle as much. The vehicles have been exchanged for modern ones and now they look very much like the trams all over Europe: practical, streamlined, but somewhat lacking in charm. The old number twelve was to be discontinued at some point in the 1980s, but after a massive protest from the by then affluent and influential inhabitants, it was saved. New tramlines are being laid in Stockholm again today, where the old ones were ripped out in the past. Finally it's been accepted that, from an environmental point of view, trams are preferable to cars and buses.

Who decides if a place is authentic? New children grow up and claim a district as their own, as the place where they spent *their* childhood. This is the world of the experiencing subject, and so, of course, *my* childhood Nockeby is the true one!

The universe of my early years was the district bordering the track of the number twelve between the square at Nockebytorg and Olovslund, where the great unknown began. It ended on one side immediately after Brålunden, a slightly dangerous place where large families were crammed into low, white blocks of flats and where, just by dint of being a child from a detached house, you could be challenged in some humiliating way; and on the other side a short distance down the quiet and anonymous little street, Nockebyvägen, with its large white rendered houses. In Brålunden there was a Sunday School; we had to descend a staircase into a basement and there we were given stickers depicting scenes from Jesus's life that we had to put in a book – that was the best bit. But I never wanted to go, because of what might happen on the way there; nasty Gun Britt could suddenly materialise from behind a corner and terrorise me.

We lived in a large wooden house on Thaliavägen, just where a steep hill – it was steep then at any rate – led down to the square. You could also walk to the square through the 'park' next to our house, but not in winter, when a large yellow sign above the steps proclaimed 'Not Gritted!' The older children in the street had created an icy sledge run which finished in an elegantly curved bank of snow that stopped tobogganists running straight into a pine tree. Crashes did happen sometimes – you would see traces of red blood on the white snow, as well as the revolting yellow dog pee.

The park wasn't designed as such; it was just a gravel trail through a small patch of wild ground between the back of the gardens and the tramline. The whole area was around 800 square metres, but it made an ideal adventure land for us. We built dens and even skied – on those short, wide skis, rounded at the front, and to which you had to attach the ski boot with a leather strap. The almost imperceptible inclines were perceived by us as slopes. In one spot there were chanterelles, which I guarded closely. When I was very young the tramway trench between Nockebytorg and Olovslund was my refuge, albeit strongly forbidden, of course. Indeed, there was an odd discrepancy in the rather erratic upbringing my parents gave me and my little brother; in many ways it was very strict, and yet for long periods of the day we were totally unsupervised and had enormous freedom. Our parents had no idea what we were actually doing in those intervals when Dad was at the Seamen's Welfare Board and Mum was confined to the big house. Nowadays young children seem to be watched the whole time; nursery and after-school club staff have a constant presence, like guardian angels.

But back to the tramway trench! That was where, in early spring, I picked the first coltsfoot, liverleaf and wild violets, which smelled as good as the violet pastilles Mum had in her bag; or where I pushed my hand in as far as it would go between the palings of garden fences and grabbed a handful of cultivated flowers – Mum was never surprised about the bouquets she received! She didn't even ask any questions when given tulips from the flowerbeds on the square (now a car park). In autumn we pilfered berries growing on branches that were sticking through the fence; Mr Levedal's huge red gooseberries were so sweet and it was so exciting to creep along the trench up to his garden – your whole body was tingling. There was always a risk that the warning bell on the number twelve would ring or that Mr Levedal, who was a pensioner and therefore ancient, would come charging out of his house, shaking his fist, shouting 'I'll show you, little miss!' You had to seize your chance in the twelve-minute intervals between trams, and it was very embarrassing when you didn't have time to duck and the driver rang his warning bell, or, woe betide you, when the number twelve simply came to a halt and the furious driver stormed out of his cab in a rage.

But I had my safe hiding places: one was behind a clump of raspberries, an offshoot from somebody's raspberry patch, where I was completely invisible to spying eyes from the tram windows, and another inside a broken fence belonging to a rather absent-minded elderly lady. This trench was no more than a metre wide, but it was mine.

And as for Thaliavägen – at that time there were so few cars passing, children could play without any trouble in the middle of the street. In winter the high piles of snow at the edges of the road were the responsibility of Birre, who had a big straw-berry nose, a steaming work horse whose muzzle was always in a sack of oats, and a three-cornered wooden snow plough. These piles were hollowed out and transformed into fortresses where war was waged with hard snowballs as ammunition. It always snowed on Christmas Eve and, after the Christmas presents had been opened and Christmas dinner eaten, Dad and I would go out, hand in hand, into the white silence.

The world I knew contained three houses below ours on the same side, five on the other side and a few more opposite, where Författarvägen started. They operated like secure strongholds, the aroma in each hall utterly distinctive (even today I would only be able to tell which one I was in by the smell) and in each of them a housewife reigned. Did the word 'housewife' exist then? There were two exceptions: Mrs Levedal, who went out for the number twelve every morning to go to work at the telephone company, and Mrs Bodecker, who also worked outside the home.

The small square with all its little shops is still there, but it has of course changed. A great deal can happen in sixty years. Prosperity has increased, as have house prices, and Nockeby, a suburb close to Stockholm city centre, is a very popular residential area, perhaps because it has retained its small-town character. It was built in the 1930s and today apartments are selling for around 60,000 kronor per square metre. In my day all sorts of people lived around the square and most of our shopping or repairs could be carried out there.

I wonder if the current occupant of the chic dress shop knows that it actually ought to be Mr and Mrs Suhr's paint shop. Mrs Suhr was always rather stern and serious, her face pale, wearing her brown spectacles and her perpetual white coat, while Mr Suhr, who always hovered in the background, wore a green coat throughout my entire childhood and had a pencil behind his ear. The shelves in the secret corners of the shop could yield all you ever needed – it wasn't as difficult to choose then as it is now. There was also a son, a young Master Suhr – think of the game 'Happy Families' – who helped out from time to time, but no young Miss Suhr.

For some reason we didn't shop at Mr Sam Larsson's (whose name obviously morphed into 'Samlarsson'); adults would unaccountably fall out with someone to whom they had hitherto been well disposed. It had absolutely nothing to do with the large box of chocolates I appropriated there – Samlarsson used to write down all your items on a piece of paper, and if you threw it away, you didn't have to pay. Or so the dentist's daughter said. With this lavish present in hand, I went to the birthday party of the doctor's daughter, Lillis, to which I wasn't invited. The result was twofold: I still wasn't allowed in and I was given a smack by Dad for the first and only time in my life.

When we bought milk in the shop next door we took our own tin containers and the milk was ladled out with a long-handled measuring spoon, litre by litre. In the adjoining butcher's shop, water would run along the window and there was sawdust on the tiled floor. It was surely more fun to buy meat and sausages and mince – minced here in the shop before the customer's eyes – from the polite Engström brothers in their slightly blood-bespattered white coats, than to buy it ready-weighed, tidied up and wrapped in plastic. I remember the grinding noise of the mechanical meat slicer and the shop assistant neatly picking up the pieces and placing them on waxed paper. And the bags you took home were flattened

65

out by Mum and put in a drawer with all the bits of string –
nothing was wasted, you never knew what might be useful.

Gradually my world expanded. I started at Olovslund
primary school and my route there, so full of adventure, went
along Thaliavägen, over the number twelve tramline in Olovslund, down through a little copse to the small wooden houses
on Västerled, and then I had almost arrived at the low yellow
school building. This is the path I walk over and over again in
my dreams.

The small cottages of Olovslund were built in the 1920s,
in a district to become densely populated with large families.
But the houses in the area around Nockebytorg and Nockeby
were designed by various different architects towards the end
of the 1930s, and built with the middle classes in mind. You
reached this garden suburb from inner-city Stockholm via
the Traneberg Bridge, constructed at the beginning of the
1930s. These two areas are among several others on the out-
skirts of Stockholm during the twentieth century that have
been described by Birgitta Conradsson in her book *Settlers
in Bromma*. According to the Stockholm city plan of 1999,
Nockeby and Olovslund are designated of cultural significance. Olovslund is regarded as an historical site of national
importance. And today these two garden suburbs are relatively
homogenous areas in terms of house owners and life styles.

When we were young we were not conscious of who was
well off and who wasn't, but we understood vaguely that there
was a difference between people. Today I think of nasty Gun

Britt, the bane of my childhood, as an example of class warfare in miniature: she turned against me, and all the other children from the large houses, because we represented something she felt excluded from. I sometimes wonder what became of her.

# Princess Cake

A pastry chef lives here in town,
Baking cakes the whole day long.
Baking big cakes, baking small,
Baking some with sugar on.

One of the most Swedish of experiences is to slip into a patisserie and order a cup of coffee, maybe with a cinnamon bun, a princess cake, or why not a punch roll. In recent years a more sophisticated type of café has appeared, especially in large towns and cities. They are filled with teenagers dressed in black, young mothers with buggies, or the occasional customer, bent over a laptop, who wants to be alone in the company of other people. Everyone sips a latte or a cappuccino, studiously avoiding the intake of anything too calorific.

But many people still seek out the genuine Swedish patisserie, the *konditori*, whose roots go back to the old cake and confectionery baker's. We're not talking here of the elegant cafés of Paris and other European cities, the exquisite delicacies on offer in the Café Sacher in Vienna or the Café Einstein in Berlin; this is a simpler Swedish variation, a rather less well-to-do country cousin. And no one counts the calories here!

The old patisseries that have remained true to their origins, and in some cases their old neon signs from the fifties, have a loyal clientele. In the town of Norberg, located within Bergslagen, the central mining district of Sweden, there is just such a classic establishment, Elsa Andersson's Konditori, which has even kept its original exterior, a yellow painted wooden facade, and its interior fittings from the 1920s. It attracts a constant stream of aficionados ordering up their favourites. The most popular is still the princess cake or a slice of the larger princess torte. The ingredients consist of a sponge bottom, whipped cream and custard covered in light green marzipan with a thin sprinkling of icing sugar and a red marzipan rose in the middle. Some prefer to munch on a 'vacuum cleaner', a green cylindrical marzipan cake, dipped in chocolate at both ends. The official name for this tasty morsel is a punch roll and – if you buy it in supermarket, that is – in the now mandatory label of ingredients, you will read that it contains a filling of almonds and punch liqueur, a coating of chocolate, and a whole list of things such as maltodextrin, dextrose, flavouring, starch, emulsifiers and preservatives. And what is worse: the punch rolls I bought on 5 February have a best-before date of 5 April ... I think I'll be going to Elsa's.

Perhaps you would rather have a Napoleon, or mille-feuille, made up of layers of puff pastry, crème pâtissière or whipped cream, and jam, glazed with icing combed with redcurrant jelly. There is also the adored Shrovetide bun, a light puffy bun made from wheat flour, yeast, salt, sugar, eggs and baker's ammonia and filled with an almond paste mixture of milk and marzipan, topped with whipped cream and a dusting of icing sugar. Talk about a calorie shock!

The range in a Swedish *konditori* is generally not extensive, but disappointment is deep if the particular cake or bun you have been looking forward to isn't there, the one that always has been. The Napoleon, for example, has been known in Sweden since the middle of the nineteenth century. It's a diverse crew that goes to Elsa Andersson's: the carpenter in his blue overalls, the old lady who insists on wearing a hat, the young mothers with their small children, the elderly former miner, and a few school pupils who dislike that day's school meal. During the summer season coachloads of retired people pour into the *konditori*, ready for a change of scenery and a chat over a cup of coffee, and we know that 'A drop of coffee is the best of all earthly drinks', as it says in the Swedish vaudeville song. Note that there is definitely nothing stronger on offer in a *konditori* – it's not the place for alcohol! But some people do prefer to drink hot chocolate with whipped cream instead of coffee, maybe after a skiing outing or as a comforting treat when the thermometer plunges to minus twenty-five. It's quite touching to see the elderly gentleman holding the string of his cake box carefully between the forefinger and thumb of his large hand, with the clear intention of sitting on his own at home enjoying his pastry in peace and quiet.

# The Battle for the Elms

Something definitive and remarkable happened in Stockholm on 12 May 1971. A large, disparate crowd of people congregated under the elm trees in Kungsträdgården, the closest you can get to the heart of the city, to protest against the cutting down of the magnificent elms round the little Tea House. The local council had decided that a new entrance to the underground and a shopping centre were to be built there, despite continuing voices of protest, including that of the national poet, Evert Taube. 'If the government and municipal councils of Sweden are allowed to persist in carrying out their acts of destruction from the Stora Sjöfallet National Park to the elm trees in Kungsträdgården ... Sweden will no longer be a civilised country. We will have become savages.'

Throughout the 1960s the spate of demolition had affected most towns and cities, especially those lacking a strong city architect. Towns that had not been obliterated by enemy bombs during the Second World War were in large parts destroyed through 'urban renewal' to the extent that people no longer recognised them. Stockholm saw the brutal demolition of seventeenth- and eighteenth-century palaces, and indeed whole areas of the city, and in Gothenburg working-class districts such as Annedal and Haga were largely razed to the ground for implementation of The Plan. The trend was seen in other Swedish towns. People felt powerless. Even the rivers of Norrland had been regulated – a fact alluded to by Evert Taube in his reference to Stora Sjöfallet; and his influence was instrumental in saving the last big unregulated river, the Vindel.

And now the colonel from Östermalm is standing shoulder to shoulder with the trendy youth from the southern suburb, people are climbing swiftly into the trees, the harsh sound of the chainsaw can be heard, a few branches are cut off, but one determined person grabs the saw, others climb onto the roof of the teahouse, a police horse falls to the ground, a 'celebrity' is dragged away, people are screaming and throwing stones, and when the protesters can see that the police and the men carrying out the felling are giving way (even the crane has retreated after an attack), a song rises up from a thousand voices: 'The elms to the people! The elms to the people', to the tune of John Lennon's 'Power to the people'.

At first the politicians in power in City Hall underestimate the force of the protesters and many of them believe that the elms will be successfully felled regardless, it is only a matter of waiting until the worst of the protest is over. Play it cool, in other words. 'It is just a question of planning to allow space for public transport', according to Hjalmar Mehr, until now the very influential social democrat mayor of Stockholm. He didn't realise that the question was much bigger than that. After less than a week the decision to fell the elms was overturned – the whole time the place had been occupied by the city's residents. The underground entrance is to be found some distance away today – it was such a good thing to build it in a less sensitive location!

The battle for the trees and for the preservation of threatened environments over the whole of Sweden continued, and many people called it simply the Battle for the Elms. This particular event spelled a distinct change in Swedish town planning and construction. Politicians in positions of responsibility could no longer arbitrarily ignore serious discontent on the part of the people. A number of places were saved that otherwise would have been bulldozed. It is precisely these 'protected' urban environments that have become extremely popular and desirable both to live in and stroll through, as can be seen in the surviving parts of Haga in Gothenburg and Gamla Brogatan in Stockholm, with their much visited cafés, restaurants, galleries and shops. In short: most people like a living city and not a glass and concrete wasteland. Now there is even scientific research to support what some of us have always vaguely suspected.

A town must live and sometimes changes are necessary. There are one or two generations of Stockholmers who have grown accustomed to the demolished and now rebuilt district in Stockholm city, where today the five Hötorg skyscrapers rise up and where the plaza commonly known as 'The Slab' or even 'The Crooked Square' (popular humour is always pertinent; this is an allusion to Stockholm's drug trade having its centre here on the obliquely shaped black and white floor tiles) extends round the tall glass obelisk, 'The Plaza Erection' in common parlance. This place is now a part of *their* native district. To recreate what was torn down in the 1960s, as has been suggested, is naturally impossible. Time heals almost all wounds, and whose city is actually the authentic one?

Stockholm: this historically fascinating and beautiful capital city, which lies at the very point where the fresh water of Lake Mälaren meets the salt water of the Saltsjön. Which is so beloved by its residents – and so maligned in the provinces, where Stockholmers are known as 'zero-eights' (alluding to the 08 area code) and described as a really stuck-up lot. The slogan 'All Sweden shall live!' has been used before several general elections, but has almost been forgotten between each. And Stockholm is growing. Some 2,163,000 people live in Stockholm County today. Gradually a new kind of class difference is emerging in Sweden, a regional one, the difference between city-dwellers and people in sparsely populated rural areas. Those thinly populated regions, including some small towns, are impoverished, to the advantage of the big cities. The well-educated move to cities, which can offer a much greater range of employment, services, entertainment and culture. One might question whether this is a development that benefits Sweden, this vast and sparsely settled land.

# A Journey over Lake Mälaren

There is a certain light associated with Lake Mälaren, a silver light, and it's only there in summer, when the scent of reeds is mixed with the scent of ripened rapeseed fields. A cement barge on its way through Galten towards Köping appears magnified against the dramatic backdrop of rain-clouds that have settled over northern Västmanland. A Danish yacht coming from Borgåsund with the wind aft raises its sails like huge wings and for a second becomes a swan. Fountains of light fall in a dramatically Dutch way over sand quarries and castle gardens.

Or, when the sun on another late summer's day emerges after constant rain, a remarkable silvery radiance illuminates the bays. A pair of great crested grebes materialises for a moment in the silver half-light; two cranes move slowly over the giant reeds by Strömsholm Palace, as if their wings are beating through a substance denser than normal air. Disused barges and the last of the lighters from the Strömsholm Canal languish solemnly in old, derelict harbours. In neglected castle gardens gooseberries ripen than no one will find.

In truth Lake Mälaren, the heart of Sweden and the great lake of Swedish literature, defies all description. I challenge anyone who claims there has ever been anything like it anywhere else in the world. According to geologists, Lake Mälaren consists of four large basins that slowly drain, one into another, with Södra and Norra Björkfjärden lowest and Galten, fed with abundant water from the rivers up in the northwest, as the uppermost level in the water's descent. It is a lake with a myriad islands. Or, rather, a landscape throughout which water has been allowed to enter, creating a special kind of environment and a special kind of culture: a water labyrinth, where early communication was more concentrated and less difficult than in other regions and where culture could therefore begin to flourish.

And it is a lake that, ever since those grey and distant times, has remained the heart of the country, with its poets, and its towns, which once all had the same characteristic oaks, willows and aspens, neat streets of cobblestones between small red and white houses, and some which even now preserve their distinctive character. And of course the castles, these wonders of red and white stone, the green patina on copper roofs, the mighty towers and cupolas that suddenly appear when you round a headland. Sometimes turned into museums, sometimes reduced to folk high schools or detox centres, they retain still today, and always will, something of their former glory. This is partly what makes Lake Mälaren the heart of Sweden, in the same way that the poets did.

Castles and cities, culture openly associated with wilderness, a garden, a water labyrinth: not even a Chinese poet in his wildest imagination could have created something like this. So how did it all begin? It's difficult to say. In *Heimskringla*, a collection of sagas about the Old Norse kings written by the thirteenth-century Icelandic historian Snorri Sturluson, Sigtuna is mentioned as the oldest of all the inhabited places by Lake Mälaren. Snorri tells of how King Olaf the Holy sails into the Baltic Sea and then on into the great lake Lögrinn (as Lake Mälaren was called by the ancients), rampaging and pillaging. A Swedish king offers resistance, and it is only with the greatest of difficulty that King Olaf's ship manages to retreat through the 'Stockesund', where heavy rain has turned the outlet into a torrent.

'*Þá váru regn mikil*' – how easy it is even today, in the rainy half-light of an August evening on the Björkö Sound, to see the long grey ship with its menacing dragon's head prow and the shadowy rowers, to hear the rhythmic sound of the long oars being raised and lowered! And the swishing noise from the bow, the smell of woollen cloaks, wet from days of rain. Out here on the site of ancient Birka, you really feel you are at the heart of the Kingdom of Svea.

Little can be seen in the August twilight of the erstwhile capital itself, which dates back to the eighth century, other than burial grounds and fragments of the ancient city walls. A cow is lowing in the late-summer dusk, lights are going on

77

in Björkö village, and over the site of the ancient city itself, in a region of 'dark earth', only peace reigns. But when you stand high-up on the cliff where the fortress stood, knowing that all the oak pilings where the ships were tied could still be seen at low tide in the nineteenth century, for a moment you have a sense of the life that was once lived here. Sometimes autumn storms can even wash up pieces of amber, long ago lost overboard on vessels transporting their load of amber from the East Prussian shores. This is perhaps the most beautiful, the most peaceful and yet the most mournful place on Lake Mälaren.

> In Upper Svealand lies the magnificent Lake Mälaren. Much of note has been reported about it before, in particular that on its shores are many fortresses and castles, belonging to noblemen and other distinguished persons, and quite imposing according to the custom of the land. In addition there are some cathedrals of distinction, such as Västerås and Strängnäs.

This is the voice of a man who in all probability had seen the place. The author of the remarkable renaissance treatise published in Rome in 1555, under the elegant Latin title *Historia de gentibus septentrionalibus: libri XXII*, was born is Linköping, but according to reliable reports spent time in both Uppsala and Strängnäs. Olaus Magnus, the man in question, author of *A Description of the Northern Peoples*, is often identified as 'our last Catholic archbishop'. This is true, inasmuch as he was appointed to this high office by Pope Paul III after the death of his brother, Johannes Magnus, in 1555, yet it had no practical bearing as his book was written in exile. Olaus was already abroad on diplomatic service at the time of Gustav Vasa's reformation and, as the clever old Owl Edition of the *Nordic Family Book* of 1914 expresses it: 'He remained abroad on account of disaffection for the growing church reformation in Sweden.'

*A Description of the Northern Peoples* is a wonderful book, with its accounts of skating trips, ancient rings broken by legendary kings on high towering rocks, and forest travellers finding their way in the depths of winter darkness by placing sticks of phosphorescent wood between the trees to mark their path. It's much more amusing than even some knowledgeable people realise, and, like many other books of exile, is imbued with deep patriotism.

However, there is a painting by Prince Eugen from 1893, which captures the characteristic magic of Mälaren castles better than words. *The Old Castle* depicts Sundby Castle, not far from Eskilstuna, on the south side of the lake. When you enter Sundby's excellent marina on a summer's day now and find your bearings in the forest of large, glamorous yachts, the magic is all still there, though the castle has become a restaurant and is rented by a folk high school. The slumber of the briar rose lingers on as it does in the dreamy architecture of Swedish and European romantic art of the 1890s.

Not all of Lake Mälaren's castles have been turned into folk high schools or clinics of one kind or another. It is true that Nordic writers and others gather sometimes for conferences in the imposing Bishop's Kitchen on Biskops-Arnö, and the Knights' Hall in Sundbyholm is hired out for weddings now and then, but aristocrats still exist around Lake Mälaren. Some even open their homes to tourists, in the same way that lords of the manor do today in England. Tidö Castle shows its library and delightful little toy museum, and the owner of Ängsö Castle will gladly regale visitors with the tale of the mysterious gold chain that can never leave the island or the castle will burn. The splendid library at Fullerö Castle is not, as far as I'm aware, open to the public. Yet somehow it still feels safe, sailing past and knowing that, over in the greenery, room has been given to kilometres of shelves filled with classics and Swedish belles-lettres.

There is something here of the same profound Mälaren atmosphere that I remember in several happy outings as a child. I was fortunate to have as a sports teacher the former artillery captain Algot Hammarsten, an officer and a gentleman who also happened to own one of Lake Mälaren's largest sailing boats (if my memory serves me right), a ketch called Dunungen that had sailed to Finland, which in those days was a remarkable feat for a pleasure craft. On the first sports day in September every year Algot Hammarsten would take a high-school class out on his boat, and these leisurely trips between islands bursting with plant life and the swims in fragrant water, still warm from August, will stay forever in my memory.

When I, one rainy August day, go rattling at twenty knots past these islands in Blackenfjärden and Västeråsfjärden, in a fast, perhaps rather too fast, and very comfortable hired motorboat, past the place where we were once becalmed and had to pull at the ketch's heavy oars, I can clearly hear the sad whisper of Gunnar Mascoll Silfverstolpe's poem:

It was then, when our pockets were bulging
With bruised fruit covered in rain-soaked mud.
It was then, when the garden lanterns were lit,
And they shone on the crayfish plate in a shaded arbour.
It was almost too cold to bathe
And cobwebs shrouded the thickets.
As the last load was taken to its store
The sky was clear and the wind blew cold.

It was those days, when we eagerly weighed
Every hour left at the end of the holiday.
It was then, when every hour possessed
The singular strength that had to be attained.

This fine Västmanland minor poet did not hail from a castle, but from the captain's residence at Stora Åsby in Rytterne parish. Noble-minded, articulate, always with a tone of solitude, Silfverstolpe managed to capture the melancholy and the enduring silvery luminosity of Lake Mälaren better than anyone I know.

How much remains today of the particular culture of the Mälaren region, of the secluded bays and undisturbed villas, glass verandas and tranquil harbours that make up the *staffage*, not just to the first chapter of Sigfrid Siwertz' *Pirates of Lake Mälaren*? A few short summer weeks of odd forays in a motor cruiser of the modern, preformed plastic type can only form the basis for a very approximate answer indeed.

With its German yachts, coachloads of American visitors and impressive tourist office, where a woman appears to be perpetually in deep conversation with a relative, Mariefred is something of a parody of the old Mälaren place it used to be. Like Fisherman's Wharf in San Francisco, it started impersonating itself long ago. The biggest attraction is the Eastern Södermanland Railway, a narrow-gauge railway that is operated in the summer months between Mariefred and Läggesta by a team of amateur enthusiasts.

However, most of the foreign tourists, especially the Germans, come here to visit a grave. For here is the resting place of Kurt Tucholsky, one of many tragic destinies in modern literature. This brilliant Berlin poet, who courageously challenged Nazi brutality, ended up here during his years in exile, in the setting of the light-hearted yet sad short novel, *Castle Gripsholm*, which he had published in 1931, a few years before his death. 'Read-write-shut up' is the melancholic essence of the life he confided to his diary. He forged no real contacts in Sweden as he headed towards despondency and suicide. There was even a theory that he was assassinated by a special commando on a mission from Berlin. On his grave, which is always decorated with fresh flowers in summertime, is a rather surprising quotation from Goethe: '*Alles Vergängliche ist nur ein Gleichnis*' – 'All that is transitory is but metaphor' – a phrase that in its noble Platonism does little to offer us solace as we contemplate Tucholsky's fate.

The wonderful town that Sigtuna still was in my childhood, with matching low wooden buildings round the perfect square, artisans' houses with yards for the stablemen's horses, tranquillity and weeping willows, can now only be experienced in poetry. The following account of a journey appears in a letter from the Uppsala Romantic Adolph Törneros to Pehr von Afzelius, 8 July 1825:

> When we emerged from the forest, the hospitable town lay a stone's below us. The houses spill over one another, like a herd of red and white cattle, and in the midst of the jumble the tower rises up like a staff to control them.

On the other hand, Strängnäs has had the sense to preserve its character and has done so better than all the other Mälaren towns: it has an idyllic atmosphere, an almost Dutch quality to the light over its streets, a majestic cathedral that is so much more than a museum. Here, under the linden trees, it is still possible in the few short hours of a summer's afternoon to dream of a Sweden that existed in the past and that for decades seems to have been destined to be buried in concrete. The remarkable thing about Strängnäs is that it feels like a living town and not a museum, something that perhaps can also be said only of Torshälla.

As I walk westward on a clear, blowy July day, in the kind of fresh wind that blows away the rain clouds of high summer and puts white beards on the huge waves in the fjords, I have an almost mystical feeling that I am going *deeper* into the country; there is a smell of Bergslagen and forest, even the water seems to take on a faint tinge of the Bergslagen lakes' rich soil. On a day like this, when the keen, biting wind sharpens all senses, it's easy to imagine the laden old ore freighters that once carried pig iron and raw material down to the railway in Stockholm from the distant ironworks on the river of Kolbäcksån. Most of them made it, having clambered down the almost endless flight of locks in the Strömsholm Canal and then laboured on through the rough swell and the raw gusts of wind on the fjords.

At Borgåsund, where water flows into Lake Freden, a change is noticeable. Between the oak trees in the north there is a glimpse of the copper roof of Strömsholm Palace, and majestic groups of riding-school horses moving through the groves of trees. But out over the vast wetlands on the other side of the bridge, in Lake Mälaren's north-westerly corner, two cranes are already migrating.

Passing from the Mälaren fjords to the canal is a breathtaking experience and well worth the effort. The twenty-six locks up to Lake Barken afford such beauty; the three famous Sörk-varn locks in Halstahammar, the instant you see them from below, when they are empty before the water is let in, resemble a strange cathedral that might actually have been placed the wrong way up, with its arches pointing downwards. To be in such close contact with the countryside is fascinating, not least in the excavated sections of the canal, where the route goes down an avenue of pretty alders and aspens. Angling fishermen and grazing cows, not to mention prolific bird life, provide constant variety. Even going through the locks themselves (which isn't as difficult as the uninitiated might fear) grants a useful exercise in contemplation, as you stand with the rope and boat hook and watch the stone structure, wet and solid, slowly sink down into the rushing water.

Unfortunately in recent summers the canal company has been foolish enough to give priority in the narrow stretches to the passenger boat 'Strömsholms Kanal', a wide, paddle-boat-like water-borne wine bar and restaurant, which blocks the excavated sections as effectively as a large-scale cork. It wouldn't be a problem if the maître d' – I hesitate to call him the skipper – hadn't regrettably failed to realise that with privileges come responsibilities. If he's an hour or so late, there is always the risk you will miss the last lockage of the day. And, according to the lockkeepers, this floating drinks veranda is never on time.

Strömsholm Canal is not as well managed as it could be and you can't be sure of getting through in the two days stipulated in the timetable. However, for anyone with time and patience it's still rewarding to make the journey along this waterway opened in 1787; for the locks, for the white-throated dippers and the swallows over the water, for the cranes that sooner or later will come in a celebration of freedom over the huge pale lakes of the north on their migration south, for the lovely, tilting old farmhouses, for the friendly lockkeepers and their happy little dogs.

When we glide out onto Lake Åmänningen through the narrow inlet of Ryssgraven bay the surface of Lake Mälaren is already ninety-nine metres below us. Here the water makes a different sound – like a mountain lake. And suddenly Lake Mälaren seems far away, beneath the horizon.

And yet the whole of this water world forms a clear and well-defined entity. I believe that Swedish literature would have been quite different without it. The winds, movements of waves and water that exist here, would have made their absence felt. Swedish culture is not least a water culture, a creation by people who have lived close to water and have understood its spirit. It's no coincidence that both the Scandinavian kings involved in the Thirty Years' War were known as the 'Water Kings'.

It is in the water of Lake Mälaren that our poetry has its origins. And it can still be found there.

# *Wetlands*

The marshland, entrance forbidden,
Dangerously deep, with purple loosestrife and pondweed.

The salamanders we caught
and called them 'newts'.

Extinct now, most likely. Who cares?
Suddenly the boy was twenty years old.

A long life lay before him
Like the Courland plain.

The brook. The salamanders.
We were the ones who took it all away.

No one else.

When I was six years old my parents moved from the west part of Västerås to what was then the east part. In the districts round the port in the west with its quays and mounds of coal, my only real contact with nature was a tiny clump of pine trees (that now looks pathetically small), squeezed in between a petrol station and a couple of blocks of flats. But back then it was a place of adventure.

Yet what was that compared with the vast expanse of woodlands that opened out for exploration after the move to Bomansgatan? This was true forest, far surpassing the fields adorned here and there with islands of boulders and conifers. And it was actually endless. The perimeter of the forest was marked by a copse of oak trees, and an idyllic little stream flowed through, too shallow to drown in, but ideal for competitions between bark boats, matchsticks or whatever else we could muster. The stream, which was called Emmausbäcken after a nearby manor house, has now for half a century run through an underground tunnel beneath European Highway E18 and all that remains of the forest is the occasional pine tree between apartment buildings. No one can possibly imagine how it once looked.

The marshes, of which there were several, are now completely drained. They were bordered by all the colourful plants that are native to wetlands such as these. And there were the salamanders, members of the extensive Urodela order of amphibians, that we used to catch and keep in jars until lack of oxygen and hunger finished them off. We didn't know they were salamanders – and presumably endangered – and we called them 'newts'. I wonder if they have survived in

Västmanland. Perhaps on the larger islands out in the Mälaren, on Ängsö, Tidö or Almö-Lindö?

The nearest marsh was where my primary school friends and I learned to skate on yellow, uneven ice with the kind of skates known as 'pokers', fastened by straps outside the boots. Mine disappeared years ago – I sold them to a school friend – but, curiously, I can still remember the feel of them against my ankles; how rebelliously and independently they rocked from side to side. Until we painstakingly learned to gain control over them. Skating is apparently one of those skills you can't forget. In the sixties I found a 'poker' in a field of potatoes in Sörby Gård in Väster Våla, a long way up in northern Västmanland. It must once have been used on the large Lake Åmänningen. Maybe in the nineteenth century, or possibly even earlier.

Marshlands and bogs are intrinsically different. They have different smells and different vegetation. You might say they have different souls. Marshes are created by a water table very close to the surface. They are edged with reeds and well-known waterland plants, such as purple loosestrife, bulrushes, water-lilies, and under the surface there are waterweeds and long trailing seaweed. Bogs consist of some flowing water, and in the forests of Västmanland they often seem to lie like a shadow round an existing lake, the gloomy older sisters of forest lakes.

Bogs can give the dangerously misleading impression that they are solid enough for you to walk on, with a tangle of tree-dominated vegetation often growing between open pools.

'Quagmire' is the perfect word for that kind of treacherous mat of mosses, plant roots and peat that gives way underfoot. At least two armies of Danish knights lie in the Hällaskogen bogs in Västmanland, and they are not likely to be seen again for a long time, the most recent being the one conquered by Karl Knutsson in 1434.

It is a strange sight when a family of elks travels over a bog. These animals, with a rhythm to their movement that reflects the countryside through which they pass, never seem to have a problem with the treacherous nature of a bog; whereas cattle that stray in are generally doomed to drown. Even a large crowd of men with ropes round their waists would be unable to save a cow that had sunk into a bog. I recall how the slowly bloating carcass of one such cow struck fear into us as small boys on our dangerous rambles in the Brattheden bog, the shadow to Lake Norra Nadden, or as it's called on old maps, Stora Nadden. Was there a latent song about flies lurking there, like Baudelaire's supreme 'Une charogne'? I don't recall. But I do recall the stench. 'Nature is good' is the slogan on a modern packet of Swedish Bregott butter. I find it hard to think of anything more crassly cynical.

There is an overwhelming smell reminiscent of a chemist's shop. There is meadowsweet, cottongrass, countless kinds of moss and lichens (when in doubt step on the dark green sort, it's always on slightly more solid ground, never on the light green) and special bogland delights. Among tussocks the frail coils of the cranberry's delicate tendrils, a fragile Arctic vine with small red berries that are said to be best if they're picked in October after the skins have been shrivelled by the first frost. The special bog bilberry, the blueberry's sombre dark blue cousin, whose large, strange-tasting berries are said to contain narcotic elements, maybe even opiates. But the ultimate berry is the golden queen of the Rubus species, the cloudberry. Not very easy to find, because they grow predominantly on raised bogs where it's difficult to walk, the cloudberry is slow to ripen, first white with streaks of red, and then, as the tender plant sucks up more flavours and sublime sugars from the earthy-smelling peat, it finally attains its definitive amber colour.

The cloudberry is in great demand. In the north of Sweden a war zone can easily develop between different berry-picking troops. Groups of Thai workers are shipped in from far-off Asia to work at a daily rate, kept in camps under slave-like conditions and duped into going home with a fraction of their earnings. (Voltaire might have said: This is the price you pay if you take cloudberry jam on your vanilla ice-cream at the Operakällaren Restaurant.) In recent years the authorities have become aware of the situation. Or so they claim.

In southern Sweden it's done in a much calmer manner. People keep their cloudberry patches secret, much more secret even than their wild strawberry patches, and they like to hide the contents of their baskets under a layer of something else, such as chanterelles, which appear in abundance at the same time. The taste of a cloudberry is one of those difficult things to put into words. Sweet, mysterious, with a sensual air of feminine wistfulness.

There are entirely different types of wetland. The mesh of reeds that flourish round the lowland lakes can be veritable labyrinths. The boats indigenous to a particular district, such as the ones I knew in the River Kolbäcksån water system, when they were still built by hand by local carpenters, are true expressions of the waters in which they are used.

My father's rowing boat, built in 1939 by a man called Bark down by Ramnäs Bruk ironworks and rowed home single-handed up to Norra Nadden and Brattheden by my dad, Einar Gustafsson – a feat that took more than three hours – was a typical example. Flat-bottomed, squared off fore and aft with simple rowlock arrangements, it is a boat that is able to enter very shallow water indeed, and can be pushed along through the reeds with a good solid pole. (This is the equivalent of punting in Oxford and Cambridge. The flat-bottomed punt is remarkably similar to a Västmanland rowing boat, only narrower and more oblong.)

For really thick reeds you took along a special scythe. You can still see them in old tumbledown boatsheds here and there. A short, relatively thick blade at the end of a long sturdy shaft or hook. You don't have to strike with a reed scythe. You thrust it into the reeds, as far under the surface as you can reach, and pull it towards you. By doing this you can create passageways through the reeds. When furthest into the reeds, you lay a hoop net or fish trap. In the spring especially, when the pike are spawning, the results can be spectacular. This labyrinthine realm of reeds is full of life in many shapes and forms. Pike thrash after swiftly vanishing shoals of small fish; there is the glint of bleak and roach. In the channels and openings sea birds, ducks and swans, marshalled neatly in pairs; the great northern diver and its mournful wail; and, of course, the great crested grebe, this wise, low-lying bird that, in common with the great poets, has embraced both worlds, of water and air.

The biologist Bengt Berg introduced the Canada goose to the Västmanland environment. Perhaps he should have resisted the temptation. There are places along the upper reaches of the Kolbäcksån, between Naddtorpet and Byggetorp, where hundreds of them fill the water-meadows. Unfortunately they're not very palatable. They have a very sharp taste. And – what's worse – they have a penchant for eating the roots of reeds. The result is that the labyrinthine waterways, channels and sky-reflecting *étangs* of my childhood have been reduced by almost fifty per cent.

Fishing in the Norra and Södra Nadden was not without its controversies when I was a child. Ramnäs Bruk manufacturers, characterised by bullying behaviour and stinginess under its then owner Kanthal of Halstahammar, waged a veritable witch-hunt against even little boys and pensioners peacefully pulling on their oars across the lake. There was constant monitoring of who was rowing and where. Which of course encouraged a bit of cheerful villainy.

A particularly invigorating sport was disposing of the logs that had found their way out of the sawmill booms and floated ashore on some suitably deserted beach. This was long before the age of the chainsaw and it involved, under cover of dusk, sawing off what could be an excellent stock of firewood for the cold autumn days, before the arrival of the omnipresent Cerberus, the forest ranger. The inspired energy exerted on such occasions by my maternal aunt's husband, Knutte, a man whose preference was for a wicker chair on a summer-cottage veranda and two ice cubes in his glass with a drop of something more besides, was awe-inspiring.

Wetland and flooded ground is not the same thing. Further to the east, from around Haraker up to Sörhörende, the northern part of the Svartådalen valley spreads out. In the summer there are just broad expanses of meadow, so wide they meet the horizon, and hay-barns and strangely old-fashioned villages, Söråhl and Ål (with a curious difference in the official spelling). To move from the industrial and residential city of Västerås up to these parts is, as a shrewd county governor once said, like moving two centuries back in time. In the spring months the narrow silver band of the river has been transformed into huge but very shallow lakes. The innumerable barns and the strangely majestic dimensions of Västerfärnebo Church bear witness to the enormous productivity of these flooded meadows.

The springtime flocks of sparrows are a reminder of Dante's Inferno:

94

And as the wings of starlings bear them on
In the cold season in large band and full,
So doth that blast the spirits maledict;
It hither, thither, downward, upward, drives them ...

Canto V, 40–43; translated by Henry Wadsworth Longfellow

Remote villages here keep their legends secret. On dark autumn nights the ghost of Curate Dufvenberg's dog still walks in Ål; and the organ in Haraker Church might easily play unbidden, without an organist, in the deep November night. And it is here, at Lake Hörendesjön, where the lowlands bid farewell; where dense forests begin, the kingdom of the lynx and wolves; where tightly packed boulder fields – assiduously indicated by warnings on the map – lead us again into Dante's world:

All hope abandon, ye who enter in!

# Landscape of Poets

It is poets who forge a landscape. A landscape without poets is a highly unusual phenomenon – even the interior of Australia has its songlines – but of course one can always find examples. It would probably be the Arctic or Antarctica, places such as Franz Josef Land or South Georgia.

A way of coming closer to a region, of understanding its distinctive character, is to walk with the poets from north to south. Very quickly we will become aware of quite marked variations between northern and southern parts and relatively slight differences on the east-west axis, as reflected very clearly in the nation's poetry. From the sparsely populated, thickly forested coniferous region of the far north, with its mountains and lakes, as we encounter in Dan Andersson's poem:

> Furthest and deepest into the boundless forest, behind
>     Archaean rocks, steeply grey,
> Beyond immeasurable, never-ending moors, where
>     deathly silence marks each day.

To the gentle Mälaren countryside with its manor houses and castles behind great avenues of trees, its relict oak forest and springtime drifts of white sloe flowers in G. M. Silfverstolpe's poem:

> I walk a path and have to pause,
> As untold splendour holds my glance.
> The flowers of home rise like a veil
> Of wraithlike butterflies in dance.

The gap might seem wide geographically, socially and, above all, poetically, but these poets are, by and large, contemporaneous. For someone intimate with the region, the gap diminishes and a connection can be seen. Dan Andersson's poem depicts the land of charcoal kilns, the silence in the depths of forests empty of people; and Silfverstolpe's impression of the silvery Mälaren light is associated with the role of water. The path is actually the ancient iron ore road as it would have looked in the 1940s; smelted with charcoal from the forest kilns, the iron was transported on the waterways down to the large lakes Mälaren and Hjälmaren and from there through a maze of fjords, tight passages and narrow channels to Stockholm, the port of shipment.

The grey harshness and the isolation in the bogs and 'never-ending moors' have an outlet, a gateway, to a brighter landscape and wide waters. Journeys of the type we have suggested, or in the opposite direction, can be found in Old Icelandic chronicles. Central Sweden has always made use of its communication network, first its waterways and later its legendary old highways – for example the one in Dalarna across Långheden to Sala, where horse-drawn carts and day labourers were transported to and from the nation's capital – and, as time went on, its railway, and finally its present-day multitude of transport means.

There was a time, let's say in the poet Vilhelm Böttinger's youth, when Örebro, Stockholm and Västerås were a long distance from each other and the cross country journey on a stagecoach would constantly be interrupted by the opening and closing of gates. Today fluctuations in prices of apartments in Stockholm have an immediate effect on the property market in Västerås. Central Sweden has opened up and expanded. Modern road links, fast and frequent trains, even to industrial towns in the north, and above all communication technology have all brought about rapid change to this region.

Yet there are still noticeable contrasts. Between the modern ways of cities like Stockholm, Västerås and Örebro and the strangely calm serenity in the upper Svartådalen valley, with its shallow bird lakes, flooded meadows, and peaceful villages with names like Ål, Söråhl and Västerbykil, there is undeniably a gulf, a divide. The countryside here, flat and green, with barns and quietly grazing herds, looks like a Dutch landscape painting from the Golden Age. But the difference is that the great Hällaskogen, which bounds this valley to the east and caused the death of Danish knights and lords in at least two separate mediaeval battles, is quite often home to bears. And in the winter of 2010 a pack of wolves was seen on the frozen Lake Hörendesjön, not far from the village of Nyhattan.

And so when you go from field to forest to water in this region, it can feel as though you are not only travelling through different countries, but also through different times. So much gives the impression of timelessness, the impression that the passage of centuries is but a scarcely audible ticking of a giant clock. In central Europe there are entire countries more homogeneous than this strangely contradictory and diverse region of central Sweden. It is harsh, like Västerbotten, and yet wears a sweet smile, like Bjärehalvön.

Stockholm, too, has its contrasts, between an urban environment, which nowadays draws tourism and trade from the whole world, and the sudden peace of the forest that starts at Järna or Sickla – the last stops on the underground. The forest is deep and wide and only the great plains, Salaslätten in the north and Närkeslätten in the south, give a sense of openness, of purposeful and prosperous cultivation over hundreds of years. This region, too, is marked by modernisation and archaism; but modernisation can sometimes be perceived as intrusive, even brutal.

The new European routes, E18 and E4, so significant for this region, score necessarily brutal lines through the landscape, leaving an old farm here and there, hanging on the edge, as though it's lost its bearings. Motorways such as the 65 and 70 go through remote areas of deserted crofts and the capercaillie's old territory. They take us, you could say, swiftly and starkly into a wilderness that we would otherwise only reach after days of strenuous hiking. But we still have a long way to go to arrive at the total urbanisation of the central and west European landscape.

When we talk about central Sweden as an acoustic environment, it's tempting to recall how sound has changed. Motorways and important highways create a new kind of noise abatement issue. But there are also places that have become so much quieter. In the 1940s, Ramnäs Bruk, by Lake Nadden in the Kolbäcksån water system, reverberated with the noise of industrial activity; the rolling mill's orchestra of clanging, the frame saws' anxious screaming. Almost all of this is gone now. It's debatable whether Bergslagen, through centuries of mining and iron industry, has ever been as quiet as it is in this new millennium. New, soundless industries are taking over from the old. Wolves and bears are returning to the north. And the wild boar is infiltrating from the south.

What will this region look like in the future, after as many years have passed as the time between Erik Axel Karlfeldt's high school years in Västerås and now? What will the equivalent be of the poetry, the ingenuity, the creativity that has characterised life here for so many hundreds of years? We must not forget the Mälaren region has been a cornucopia of Swedish invention for two or three centuries. It was in Eskilstuna that the adjustable wrench, 'the Swedish key', was created by an ingenious blacksmith. And it was in Västerås that the three-phase alternating current first passed through a copper conduit in Jonas Wenström's laboratory. There are many more examples. Europe's share in world economy is considerably smaller today than it was in the nineteenth century when mining and iron industries dominated central Sweden; now only a fifth, compared with a third in 1870, if we are to believe the brilliant historian Niall Ferguson. It is in that context that the region will have to live up to the demands of the future.

As in so many other situations, it is intellectual and cultural resources that will be crucial, rather than natural resources. Not just Stockholm, but places such as Västerås, Köping, Örebro and Karlstad, all have rich cultural traditions. There is something often puzzling about cultural prosperity, or its absence. Places that can outwardly appear fairly comparable, for example Gothenburg and Malmö, can be of quite different magnitudes on the literary map.

The region of central Sweden is unique – thanks to its artistic, literary and technological culture.

# Old Roads

On the east side of the lake where I spent most of my summers as a child there was an unremarkable gravel road. And right next to the milk stand, where you could have a clean container filled up every day in exchange for the ironworks' milk coupons, there was a milestone: a mile and a half.

'I am a milestone from Charles XI's time', says a milestone like this in one of Hjalmar Gullberg's patriotic poems, thereby prompting an interesting discussion on philosophy of language, for another occasion.

This was the old main road between Ramnäs and the ironworks at Seglingsberg, continuing to Virsbo, where it came to an end and where journeys in summer continued by boat and in winter by crossing the ice. Sometimes the old road can still be seen from the new one, rather like an overgrown embankment, a slight elevation in the undergrowth. Every so often the new road joins the old; and from time to time you can see an ancient stone bridge with arches right next to the road you're on.

I don't really know why the former road, and its shadowy existence beside the new one, fascinates me; perhaps because it's the past made visible. In northern Bohuslän, by Torp's old school in Backa, very close to the Norwegian border, there's an old village road. It twists and turns dramatically, like old Bohuslän roads always do, in contrast to the unswerving line of the sophisticated, computer-calculated motorway that cuts through the countryside.

This old road is special. If popular belief is true, then it is the road along which Charles XII's body was carried after his death at the Fredriksten fortress. And even if it remains to be proved by maps from the first decades of the eighteenth century, it is nevertheless fascinating.

Along Barton Creek in Travis County, Texas, there's a footpath that follows the course of the creek. You meet the occasional cyclist on a mountain bike and the odd school party, here to learn about the elegant dance of the grass snake in water and the lively explosions of the touch-me-not plant. In a few places the limestone comes to the surface and it's a surprise to see the deep grooves created by centuries of wagon wheels.

Can that be right? Barton Creek, now a popular bathing spot, was the site of one of the original missions on the Spanish colonial highway, *El Camino Real*. In other words, people lived here long before the area of upper Austin was entered in the land registry. Is it possible that the loaded wagons bearing the king's imports and exports, accompanied by heavily armed riders dressed in cuirasses, once rolled along here?

We don't need to look so far afield. If we were time travellers who could visit Närke or Västmanland in the eighteenth century, we would struggle to find our bearings, because the road system would seem so inadequate, so unobtrusive, hidden so discreetly in the landscape. In her letters Selma Lagerlöf mentions not once, but several times, how she avoids the journey from Mårbacka, in Sunne, to Stockholm, because she doesn't trust the roads during the spring thaw.

The old roads represent a way of dealing with space quite unlike our own. Peace and war, love and hate, philosophy and stupidity – everything must look different in a world where it takes a week to get from Sunne to Stockholm.

Or – might I be wrong? It's worthy of debate!

# The Weather in Sweden

Let's begin by eavesdropping on a conversation between two residents of the city of Örebro, which is situated in the middle of Svealand, with 100,000 inhabitants, and which also lies at the centre of what is known as the 'whining belt'.

A: 'Nice weather today.'

B: 'Today it is, yes.'

It's unlikely to be the case that all the people who live in and around Örebro are more crotchety than in the rest of Sweden. After all, it's difficult to measure attributes of this kind in a satisfactory way. But the falling tone of the dialect can sound rather like a whine. In the example above, B could be viewed as quite well versed in scepticism – at least as far as the weather is concerned.

Swedes have a very complicated relationship with the weather. Small wonder, considering how changeable it is! It's probably the most common topic of conversation between Swedes – you can connect with someone totally unknown, if you begin a conversation on the bus, in a shop or in some other public place with: 'Today the temperature must be a record low', 'At last the sun is showing itself', or 'The heavens have certainly opened today'. A common though not very inspired response to the last remark would be: 'Yes, but down it has to come'. The rain, that is.

During the unusually cold winter of 2010 to 2011 the temperature varied from a few degrees in Skåne, in the most southerly part of Sweden, to minus thirty in central Västmanland *at the same time* – our country undoubtedly stretches a long way. Newspaper headlines warning 'ICY CONDITIONS OVER THE WHOLE COUNTRY' are hardly reliable. It was classed as the coldest December for a hundred years and Skåne alternated between periods when it was covered in snow and when it was under water as the snow rapidly thawed. Class 1 weather warnings were issued again and again for parts of Sweden – motorists advised not to venture out on the roads unless the journey was essential. There were numerous cases of cars skidding off icy roads; a woman got stuck in the snow on a minor forest road and wasn't found for a month. From the helicopter, sent out in search, the snowed-in car looked like a small undulation in the blanket of snow.

In Stockholm you needed to have your eyes *up*, in case an icicle or avalanche was about to land on your head, and also *down*, so you didn't slip on a treacherous patch of black ice. Accident and emergency departments were full of broken wrists and legs. The rest of Europe also suffered a dreadful winter that year. Those predictors of global warning who pointed with an air of superiority to the last two exceptionally

106

cold winters were confusing weather with climate, which is something else entirely.

Despite the weather, the average Swede would rather live here than anywhere else, even if more and more people fly to the Canary Islands and Thailand to escape the worst of the slush and winter darkness. Most people really love this variation in the seasons and appreciate that there is such a difference between them.

The best beginning to the Swedish weather year is a crisp, cold January day, the light already giving hope of spring. The great tit takes up his spring songs immediately after the winter solstice and other birds soon follow suit. In February, the coldest month, Swedes devote themselves to skiing and other winter sports, but in the thaws of March they delight in the first tender spring flowers next to a cottage doorstep or on a bank. April is a month known for its unsettled weather; 'April weather' implies something unreliable or erratic, when snow and spring warmth alternate in no real order. Erik Axel Karlfeldt (1864–1931, who was awarded the Nobel Prize posthumously in 1931) wrote about April:

Nothing compares to expectation,
The time for spring floods and for budding.
No May sheds a light
As bright as that of April.
Walk on the path's last slipperiness,
And add thereto the forest's musty coolness

And its deep whisperings.

Perhaps you have to be Swedish to understand how faithfully the poem renders our experience of the transition from winter to spring.

At the beginning of May the buds burst, the hallowed warmth is here, the birds rejoice and Swedes want to rejoice too and give themselves up to nature, if only they weren't so inhibited. You have utter sympathy with the shoemaker who put up a sign saying 'Closed between bird cherry and lilac', the most wonderful time of early summer. The Swedish summer, though so short, *is* wonderful, if it isn't washed away in rain, that is. In July, at the height of summer, most Swedes take a holiday. Children are off school and everyone who can goes to the beaches, both by the sea (to the west, south and east of Sweden) and around all our lakes. It's even perfectly possible to bathe in the centre of Stockholm now. There is *almost* one lake for every person; the combined surface area of all small and large lakes makes up nearly a tenth of the total area of Sweden.

In August the air is clear and summer is perfect – but the saying goes that Lars, whose name day it is on the 10th, 'throws a cold stone in the water' and the evenings suddenly become cooler. September is harvest time, 'Try to remember the kind of September, when life was slow and oh so mellow ...' and in October the snow might start coming down while the leaves are still falling from the trees. In November we prefer to stay inside as the autumn storms howl round our doors. December is dark, snow covers most of the country, but then Swedes light candles or fires to vanquish the powers of darkness, or wrap up warm and go out, to return with red glowing cheeks. Or slip and end up in the health centre. From our earliest years we have it drummed into us that 'there's no such thing as bad weather, only the wrong clothes'.

How can someone who has not been accustomed since childhood to the darkness of northern Sweden manage to survive a harsh winter there? It is dark between November and February, the sun appearing for just an hour or two in the daytime. A resident of Gällivare answered this question by saying that, in fact, it wasn't really dark – the chalk-white snow illuminated everything – and it was counterbalanced by summer, when it was light all the time in the land of the midnight sun.

But the year turns after the winter solstice on 22 December; minute by minute the days grow longer and lighter – and it all begins again!

The weather *does* something to us Swedes. Someone close to me, a poet, philosopher and present-day intellectual, is an excellent example of a typically Swedish man with an intense and deeply personal relationship with weather and wind. A rough estimate would suggest that maybe a third of the poet's daily musings and pronouncements are to do with the weather, its causes and effects. Different weather conditions are often compared with the poet's experiences of weather during his long, hard-working life, including weather he has lived through in that vast country to the west, above all in Texas. In thunder and lightning, when the person writing these words is feeling rather anxious, sitting unprotected in the middle of the fjord in Hörendesjön fishing for perch, the poet will exclaim: 'Ha! You should have been in the thunderstorm we had in Austin on 1 September 1987, when roofs were torn off houses and lightning struck the huge oak in front of our house and split it in two. *That* was a thunderstorm!' Every weather forecast is listened to carefully and informed comments made. When the temperature falls below zero outside the poet's cosy study in Stockholm's Söder district, he bursts out, with a look of longing in his eyes, 'It's a warm spring day in Austin, thirty degrees today!'

On certain days the poet refuses to go out at all, claiming that it's either too cold or too warm, or that there's not enough sun or it's too strong. He also believes he can predict the weather – he maintains he can clearly feel in one leg that a deep low pressure system is on its way. This was, in fact, just announced on the weather forecast too, but you have to take a gentleman at his word.

The thermometer outside the window is read every morning, remarked upon, and the result compared with the temperature on the same date the previous year – the poet has an exceptional memory for different weather. If it rains when he had intended to go for a little walk, he takes it as a personal insult. The only problem is, he's not sure to whom he should address his complaints.

# Ängelsberg-Västerås-Stockholm

On platform 1a at Västerås Central Station there are some wooden benches for waiting travellers. There is a piece of wood missing from the second seat on the third bench east of the station building. There's nothing remarkable about that. You can still sit on it. It's just that the piece of wood has been missing for the last three years.

I often wonder if I'll see it repaired in my lifetime. The growing, almost Russian, decline around the stations run by SJ, Swedish State Railways, and its sister company Banverket, Swedish Rail Administration – who has not noticed the strange rising mountains of rubbish surrounding the buffers for trains arriving from the north at Stockholm Central? – is in striking contrast to the increasing orderliness on the Västerås-Fagersta-Ludvika line. Platforms are being widened, and the magnificent flowering tubs at Ängelsberg station are a sign that this is somewhere special.

The nicest thing about the Ludvika-Fagersta-Västerås line, apart from the occasional spectacular views over the constantly changing surface of the great lakes, are all the young people who board the train between seven and eight in the morning in Virsbo, Ramnäs and Surahammar, on their way to high schools in Hallstahammar and Västerås. These are the young elite of Västmanland, the ones who will be running design agencies and businesses. The boys are tall, oafish, lively, the girls cheerful, endlessly texting. It gives a comical impression: they are all communicating, but not with each other, most of them with people who aren't there.

Everything written on the internet is open to the whole world. And everything said into a cordless phone on a train is also public. What are they talking about? All sorts of things. You don't put everything you pick up into print. Marcel Proust knew that, even though, according to folklore, he used to give waiters very large tips in exchange for reporting what was being said at the next table. They talk a great deal about their courses and their teachers, just as we did in the bygone fifties, on the yellow railcar between Enköping and Uppsala. A phrase I catch many times – I think it must be in fashion as the moment – is 'absolutely priceless'. The course is absolutely priceless, the lab experiment where the speaker burned his finger was absolutely priceless, the concert wasn't worth the money and was absolutely priceless.

It is very noticeable how freely these energetic young people travel across the country, from Ängelsberg to Västerås and often on to Stockholm, between home, school and recreation. These are not country yokels, and they're not city dwellers either. They are of a new sort. There are people in

Västmanland who can be described as provincial, for example if from the ancient villages in the Svartådalen valley, Ålsvärta, Nyhattan, Västerbykil. But these young people don't belong there. They travel in a wider space than we did. They are in motion, and fundamentally they are moving away from the woodlands, from the bogs and from the great, calm lakes.

The bishop of Västerås diocese, Claes-Bertil Ytterberg, an old acquaintance whom I meet today at lunchtime in the queue for the hot-dog stand on Stora Torget in Västerås, once told me how impressed he was as a little boy when he was allowed to take the bus from his home in Surahammar into Västerås, *where the streets were paved*.

# Norberg

In the northern part of Västmanland on the border with Dalarna lies the friendly, well-kept little town of Norberg, musing over its former glory days, when it was an important hub for the iron industry. Perhaps one should say 'municipality', that's its bureaucratic title. But I persist in using the word 'town'; and besides, Norberg is one of the oldest in Sweden. Norberg is marked on some trade route maps from the Renaissance – and Stockholm isn't!

We live in Norbergsån, the town's historic centre, with beautiful old wooden buildings, mostly painted in traditional Falun red. The original market place, bustling with so much activity in the past, is, of course, a car park now, for people who work or have business at the town hall; the grey concrete facade of this sixties' building, which would have fitted very well into a German town in the GDR, is now regarded as architecture typical of its time and is subject to a preservation order.

Near to this modernist creation are several of the handsome old manor houses with barns and outhouses that belonged to mine-owners, and down by the river there are wash-houses, exactly as they looked in earlier times. In the barn closest to our house there's a staircase leading down into a vaulted cellar, thought to be from the fifteenth century, very close to the church. Perhaps, deep in the earth beneath, there is a connection to the church, whose vaults were in existence in the fifteenth century. Intriguing, and not impossible. In any case, you can speculate about the nature of the ground you're walking on here – Norberg is like an upside-down Manhattan, when you think of all the mine tunnels and underground rooms beneath you in this area. Mining was already in practise in the Middle Ages. According to the Swedish National Encyclopaedia there is evidence of forty foundries, ten or more hammer works, and hundreds of pits here.

The Falun copper mine and Sala silver mine are both relatively close. In fact, the reason the mine-owners' old houses in Norberg are painted red (the well-known trademark is Falu Rödfärg) is due to the pigment that was extracted as a bi-product in the mining of copper at the Falun mine. This red colour made a big impact: it can be seen on many wooden buildings, both houses and barns, all over Sweden.

No more than two hundred metres from where we live you can find most of what you need for daily life: two well-stocked shops, which perhaps could compete a little more with each other when it comes to price-setting, a chemist's, the government-owned off-licence (Swedes are not trusted to buy wine and spirits in ordinary grocery shops), and Elsa

Andersson's famous *konditori*, with its nineteenth-century furnishings intact – oh, so Swedish – and where people slip in and indulgently fill up on mouth-watering Princess cakes with green or pink marzipan, or during Lent on Shrovetide buns. A quintessential Swedish story: a large, puffy bun with almond paste, cream and icing sugar. Now and then a coach-load of pensioners pour in to the *konditori* to give in to what might be their only remaining vice: coffee and almond tarts or cinnamon buns.

It's not often a new business starts in Norberg, but it has successfully happened in one of the town's most beautiful buildings, Näbbgården, in the town's historic centre. There's a small bakery there now, where the most delicious loaves are baked. Evelyn's bakery stays open while there's still a supply of bread, but her home-baked delicacies ('keep an eye on the sourdough', it says on a piece of paper at the counter) go as soon as they come hot out of the oven. A couple of days a week soup is also served by Evelyn, who always has rosy cheeks from the stove – it's very peaceful sitting in her little bakery, with the smell of baking bread, butter spread thickly on a fresh slice, savouring the soup and having a chat with the other customers.

Add a fully-stocked second-hand bookshop, a library, a craft centre full of handicrafts by mostly local artists, a gallery in Abrahamsgården, the traditional Engelbrekt Inn (there was a tavern here in the seventeenth century) with a smorgasbord in the restaurant on Sundays – and what more can you want? Well, maybe something for the soul; there's a church as well in

116

the middle of town and it's open every day to visitors, unlike most of the more rural churches. There you can sit for a while, light a candle for the dead, and reflect on the mysteries of existence. There is one additional thing, a little oddity: Norberg is teeming with ladies' hairdressers – it's obviously vital to have good hair these days, but otherwise the people of Norberg don't seem particularly vain. In this formerly industrial community, if anything, the rule is to be inconspicuous, not to stand out too much. On the other hand, those of us who come from the big city appreciate the quite special habit that Norberg people have of almost always greeting everyone they meet, including strangers. Little children can stop in the middle of a game and say 'Hello' when you walk past. It's very cheering.

And anyone who loves skiing can happily go to Norberg to practise his sport. There are numerous ski runs of varying levels of difficulty and length. One morning, late in March, the world looked wholly born anew. A little snow had fallen during the night and was lying like icing sugar on top of the rest of the snow, now somewhat tired and dirty; the sky was sunny and cloudless – it was a perfect day for skiing. We chose a track that goes past four lakes and through a forest. In deference to our age we stopped at the point where the track goes steeply uphill – where we eagerly devoured the oranges we'd brought with us – and turned back. Never does an orange taste better, and nothing tastes better than an orange, when you stand with your face turned to the sun in the great silence. Isn't this a clear example of mindfulness, the latest trend?

Pleased with ourselves, we took it rather more slowly on the way home; the only sounds we heard were the ski poles creaking, the rather disdainful cawing of a crow, and the occasional twittering of one spring bird or another. There was a distinct smell of wood smoke in the fresh air. We were in luck: in the newly fallen snow we could clearly see the tracks of a lynx next to the ski trail. These beautiful, timid animals can sometimes be seen nearby around Håberget.

Norberg is a sleepy little place nowadays; its population curve is on the way down (some 4,000 inhabitants in the town itself and 5,000 in the municipality). But perhaps this will change soon: several old mines are being reopened in Sweden and there are many companies seeking permission to prospect for ore over the whole of the country. The automotive industry in China, for example, is expanding greatly, so, who knows, maybe Norberg is heading for a golden age?

# At Elinore's Bakery in Norberg

In Norberg, early one morning in May,
The scent of lime blossom and elderflower
From mature trees next to the old house
Floats, weightless, on the smell of new-baked bread.

Beneath us there lies iron, great quantities of iron,
Mighty fields of ore,
Countless dormant particles
Silently turning the compass point.

The world comes out as soon as night is over
And undergoes hushed changes,
But someone must be there at sunrise
To knead soft dough with steady hands.

The wave of heat released
When the oven door is opened
Is the youngest descendant of the white dust
Spewed from the long-since decayed blast furnace.

The world withstands bleak transformations,
Iron can be made into swords or hammers.
Many swords or many hammers.
Countless deaths or ample bread.

# Saint Lucia

Sankta Lucia, brightest of visions,
Spread through our winter night
The shine of your beauty.
Dreams with the sigh of wings
Foretell for us miracles.
Light your white candles,
Sankta Lucia ...

It is absolutely dark this winter morning, except for the dim light cast by the snow outside – more has just fallen and lies in a white blanket, a few centimetres thick. A few snowflakes float gently down. It's half past five and we're lying alert and expectant – will Lucia be here soon with her star-boys, her girl attendants and the Christmas elf? We hear a low 'shush', some rattling of china, and detect the unmistakable aroma of coffee – we duck back under the duvet and pretend to be asleep. The door opens, a flash of light and an adorable little troop of figures with candles enters the room, singing Sankta Lucia. We sit up in bed and are so moved when we see the little Lucia with lighted candles in a crown of lingonberry twigs on her head, her long blond hair loose on her shoulders, wearing a full-length white dress with a red sash tied in a bow round her waist. She stares into the room, not looking directly at us, mesmerised with the solemnity of the moment. Lucia holds a tray in front of her, bearing coffee and cups and a plate of ginger biscuits and saffron buns. Around her stand her three attendants, also dressed in white, with sliver tinsel in their hair and round their middles, each carrying a candle in her hand. The red-haired star-boy has on his head the requisite white pointed paper hat with three gold stars. And a white night shirt. His hat is obviously rather awkward and has slipped down over one ear. In one hand he is holding a stick with a star on the end, and in the other a lighted candle. Serious, for once.

A very small elf with a red hood is sitting next to Lucia and trying his best to sing along with the words. The cat sneaks in – she doesn't seem bothered when it comes to the verse about cats, she wants to be there anyway. One more song to hear, 'Stephen was a stable-boy', with its refrain 'We all give thanks so gladly'. The children sing so beautifully, their voices clear and pure; as it will transpire, when they are adults, three of them will sing in a choir. But, turning the clock back again, at the moment Lucia is eleven, her attendants a few years younger, the star-boy is no more than seven and the elf is four.

After the singing the atmosphere reverts to a more relaxed normality; Lucia serves us coffee in bed (lukewarm, but coffee nevertheless), we congratulate them and thank them profusely, and soon they are all in our bed, chattering away, tickled pink with their performance, and the ceremonial mood has gone, just like the winter night. This was their third and last Lucia visit that morning. Now we all have to go to work, or school or nursery, where another Lucia celebration of a more official nature will take place.

It is my sister who has gathered the young cousins together and showed them what to do, to the great delight of my two brothers who live with their families in the same apartment block and who received a similar wake-up from Lucia. I am quite relieved not to have had a visit from my high school pupils who have a habit of coming to sing for their teacher before they go to school; they've been up all night and they are usually enveloped in an alcoholic haze. It's obviously amusing for them to see their teacher in her nightdress; their teacher's husband is usually less amused. Kind of them to come, but also rather trying. The feast of Lucia is on 13 December and, along with advent, is the start of Christmas celebrations in Sweden. It has Swedish roots, but most unusually it is a saint, Lucia, the patron saint of Syracuse in Sicily, who is associated with this Swedish feast. Protestant Sweden no longer has any of the saints of Catholic countries.

A few steps further back in history, in old agrarian society, 13 December was seen as a night of danger. In the Julian calendar Lucia occurred at the same time as the winter solstice, the darkest night of all here in Scandinavia. But when the Gregorian calendar was adopted in the eighteenth century, Lucia wasn't the longest night anymore; 22 December was the date when the winter solstice or midwinter occurred. In folklore, however, the tradition persists that 13 December is the darkest day of the year. On Lucia night everyone was supposed to stay indoors, give a little extra food to the animals (who on this particular night were said to have the power of speech) and try to avoid the supernatural forces that were let loose. But young people would often go out in groups to have a bit of fun, to scrounge some brandy, or similar, and also to wander around the farmsteads singing. A person of the twentieth or twenty-first century cannot really imagine how intensely dark it was in rural Sweden before the age of electricity. In all this darkness it's not strange that people believed in spectres such as wicked supernatural beings or that, during Lucia, they had to try to conjure up the powers of light so that it would return. The female figure of light *might* have some connection with a pagan goddess of light, pre-dating Christianity. Lucia comes from the Latin *lux*, meaning 'light', and the name Lucia means 'the bright one' in Sicily.

Quite a number of the Nobel laureates who stay on in Stockholm for a few days after the prize-giving ceremony on 10 December and remain in the Grand Hotel, with its fine old traditions, have spoken of their initial terror swiftly turning to delight when they were woken by a beautiful woman in a long white dress, with candles in her hair, floating into the room with her attendants, singing sweetly and bearing coffee. Lucia is celebrated over the whole of Sweden, in almost all workplaces, schools, nurseries, hospitals and old folks' homes – a consistent way of celebrating began to take shape in the first half of the twentieth century. Nowadays celebrations are very democratic; it's no longer only the blondest, most beautiful girl in the class who has the chance to be Lucia – she's usually elected. At nursery all the children are allowed to be what they want, so there can be several Lucias, including boys, as well as all the girl attendants and star-boys and elves and the recent addition of a gingerbread character. All the mums and dads, grans and granddads are invited and make up the teary-eyed audience, recording their little darlings, before heading home infused with pre-Christmas spirit. In schools it's often difficult to persuade the boys to take part in the Lucia procession. They think the pointed star-boy hats make them look ridiculous. We know how sensitive masculine pride can be, and so everyone is very grateful to the few who dare – their contribution to the singing is appreciated. 'Stephen was a stable-boy', the old ballad, part of the treasury of Lucia songs, calls for male voices too:

Stephen was a stable-boy
We all give thanks so gladly
Five steeds he watered to give joy
All for the star of brightness
Dawning light is not yet seen
The stars in the heavens they twinkle ...

When the Lucia procession has sung all the verses of their song, they slowly leave us. And all that's left are a few drips of candle wax on the floor and some tinsel. The winter's day begins to break and the year will soon be at its turn.

# Sweden's Forests

With great sadness – and suppressed anger – I recall my beautiful hall of pillars, a forest where for over thirty years I roamed, listened to the silence, found peace and also adventure, for the most part concerning wild animals, traces of earlier human life and treasure troves of mushrooms. To reach it I drove along winding, hilly gravel roads, past little red crofts and smallholdings, and then, full of expectation and equipped with basket and knife (but no compass – there has to be some excitement after all), I ventured along a maintained path into the forest. I climbed down towards a stream and then up again – this area was intersected by deep ravines that often had streams running along the bottom. Many a time there were hoof-marks in the wet earth and sometimes you could even see where the mighty elk has slipped in the mud. I was surrounded by majestic trees, mostly firs, some pines and some deciduous trees – a large grouse might suddenly shatter the silence, vigorously beating its powerful wings as it rose up directly in front of me. My basket quickly filled with different types of edible mushroom, the chanterelle predominating. I knew exactly where to look to find my mushrooms.

And now this forest has gone. In my lifetime it will not look again the way it did for almost the entire second half of the twentieth century, and it probably never will. The place has been ravaged by a violent storm, or a war, in the form of deforestation, now universal in Sweden. Of the babbling brook where I dipped my hand in to drink the water, there remains a wretched puddle. Where clear-cutting takes place, the moisture dries up and the balance of nature is disturbed. The trees are cut level with the roots; stumps, some of them seventy centimetres in diameter, are all that remain. There is still no greenery emerging and grey undergrowth surrounds the small fir trees that have already been planted in close, straight rows. Yet no ground preparation seems to have been undertaken; in forestry sites correctly prepared the ground looks as though the soil has been ploughed and can apparently be seen in satellite images. The timber has already been taken away and you can see the deep scars made by the huge forestry machines that can fell, lop and cut trees into measured logs in thirty seconds, while the lumberjack sits safe and warm in his cab – we don't begrudge him that. The cleared area is about seven hectares, so a very modest clearing. At the edge of it are uprooted trees, lying with their enormous roots exposed. In Norrland there are examples of contiguous clearings that together make up an area equivalent to ninety football pitches. I wonder how much the landowner actually received in return for letting some

128

logging contractor take 'my' forest. So much destruction for probably a negligible sum! Trees used to be felled according to their age and maturity; it was called selective thinning. It was often the owner of the forest himself who carried out this work in winter, usually with the help of a horse, which, in contrast to forestry machinery, does not damage the ground. Now they take it all, lock, stock and barrel, in one go. A planted tree in this area is considered mature for felling at an age of around seventy years. When an area of forest has been cleared and the ground prepared, firs or pines are planted tightly together. The trees will be exactly the same size and the ecology of this particular forest totally disturbed.

But there are so many forests in Sweden – can't I simply choose another one in which to pick my mushrooms or my berries? One that hasn't been cleared yet? Half of Sweden is covered by forest, after all! We have frankly never had so much forest in Sweden as now, according to the forestry industry. Yes, but what kind of forest? ask researchers as well as hikers. For we have never had such species-poor forest. Swedish forest is becoming – no, it already *is* – an industrial forest, a production forest, intended to be cut down and slung into the jaws of a sawmill. Instead of a natural forest, with different sorts of trees of varying ages, we've been given fir tree plantations, where all the trees are of equal size. And it is happening at a furious pace. Gigantic sawmills are being constructed, one after the other. Forestry is of the utmost importance to the Swedish economy. The value of our exports is more than 120 billion Swedish kronor per year – over half of Sweden's exports come from forestry. Swedish deforestation methods are even being sold to Russia. In this case we really can say: Follow the cash!

In my opinion and that of many others, it would be better to let the forest seed itself after being cleared, than to follow the brutal felling with planting and the monoculture that results. If the forest seeds itself, at least the odd deciduous tree will find a space to live; if we don't weed them all out, that is. Indeed, the administrative body responsible for forests in Sweden, the Swedish Forest Agency, has recently sounded the alarm: planted forest is not being thinned to the extent that was pledged by the landowner when permission was given to fell – any hiker in the forest can see this, because it's impossible to penetrate. And what would he do in there anyway?

But what is really serious is that we are also rapidly getting rid of old-growth forest, forest that should be protected, both as an unsurpassed place for human beings to spend their leisure time, but above all so that biological diversity can have a chance. It's dangerous to disturb the balance of a whole eco-system. Paradoxically, we express our outrage, quite rightly, at what is happening in the Amazonian rainforest, whilst we chop down our own forests with gay abandon, even original natural forests that have never been cleared. In percentage terms Sweden has felled much more primary forest than Brazil! I see that in 2011 the World Wildlife Fund suggested that Swedes should give as a Christmas present the 'adoption' of an exotic animal, such as a tiger or a gorilla, in order to protect the forests these animals need as their habitat. It would be good if, in Sweden, we could also consider adopting a white-backed woodpecker or some other creature whose numbers have been reduced to just a handful, because we have destroyed their habitats with our deforestation.

In 1992 Sweden signed the UN Rio Declaration on Environment and Development and, like many other countries, determined to take measures to protect biological diversity. We undertook to preserve around seventeen per cent of our forests. According to the Swedish model we have to keep particularly old trees, leave some woodland around streams and waterways, and preserve any historic works in the forests produced by human labour, such as charcoal kilns and dry-stone walls. Maintained paths should be reinstated. Forests are not just nature, they are culture too.

Freedom with responsibility should apply to deforestation; the environment must be taken into account. That is the basis of what is stated in the Swedish Forest Agency's paragraph 30. But what happened? The goal of seventeen per cent cannot possibly be reached by 2020, which was the agreement. Those who want to protect the forests in Sweden believe that forestry companies and some private forest owners have taken liberties and ignored responsibilities. Ironically, if an individual walking in the forest happens to pick a protected plant, a rare orchid or even a few hepaticas, he can be prosecuted, but a forest owner can destroy land with countless protected species without being fined.

There *are* forests in Sweden protected by the state, so-called nature reserves, and original forests are afforded some protection too. But not even one per cent of Swedish forest is properly protected. We have 22.7 million hectares of productive forestland, but only 727,000 hectares receive state protection and 1.2 million are voluntarily set aside by private owners. Up to now. In contrast to countries abroad where most forest is owned by the state, the situation is reversed in Sweden. Here most of it is owned by forestry companies, including multi-nationals, and individuals. The current government's reduction of 150 million in the budget for purchasing forest requiring protection is especially problematic. The Environment Minister's justification: 'We are not going to reach the environmental objectives and compulsion is out of the question. We have to think again!' We might quietly ask ourselves: How?

Every time a forestry contractor 'happens' to cut down a protected forest or clear an area around someone's house, which certainly provokes big headlines in the newspapers, they say: Oops, it was a mistake. But nothing happens. To date no one, no one at all, has been fined for a violation of paragraph 30. A parking offence, on the other hand, is something you won't get away with! Paragraph 30, about the voluntary basis of Swedish forest management, is clearly exceptionally ineffective. Even officials in the Swedish Forest Agency are of this opinion.

There is something very dishonest in the way the Forest Stewardship Council (FSC) certification, the forestry companies' own eco-labelling system, is used in Sweden. The system is international, 'voluntary and global'. All the large Swedish forestry companies boast that they are environmentally friendly; their FSC logo is printed on nappies, serviettes, and even IKEA furniture. Much of this is exported abroad. But report after report, from, for example, the Swedish Society for Nature Conservation or Greenpeace, demonstrates that FSC-certified companies often break the rules. A further paradox is that FSC-certified companies in Sweden select their own assessors ... On several occasions these companies have clear-felled key habitats, but no Swedish company has, hitherto, lost its certification. They've been reprimanded, they've promised to mend their ways – and on they go.

In 2011 the Swedish forestry industry was rocked by a scandal. The Forest Agency in Dalarna had decided to release a report to the media, and thus to the public, in which statistics showed that almost half of the felling carried out in the province failed to comply with criteria for environmental concerns. Pines over 250 years old had been cut down, for example, trees that were obviously protected. But after a telephone call from a top forestry company director, the Director General of the Forest Agency stopped the report ... This made the Agency officials hit the roof and write a letter of protest. It's odd that in Sweden it's rarely the authorities who protect the forests, but often informed members of the public, for instance, members of groups such as Protect the Forest or the Swedish Society for Nature Conservation, who try to defend untouched forest

133

areas or particularly significant ground or report alarming stories to the newspapers. There is one way to prevent this devastation and that is to find a red-listed species in a forest; that is, a species at risk of complete eradication if its habitat is not preserved. The list is established by the Swedish Environmental Protection Agency and the University of Agricultural Sciences at Uppsala, who also recommend action programmes and management plans that can be formulated for threatened environments and habitats. In this way many a forest in need of protection has been saved – a mushroom, a little insect or a moss has been discovered with the right to a continued existence!

Today in Sweden there are no more 'Seven-Mile Forests' of the old sagas, equivalent to the Hundred-Acre Wood of English literature. They are even felling in forest areas near to mountains, where trees take a *very* long time to grow to maturity. Every three hundred metres there are tracks for timber transport in the Swedish forest. Elk hunters in Dalarna, which many foreigners think of as the most Swedish of landscapes, complained that of the ten elks they were permitted, they could only shoot four – there was too little forest, and too much clear-cutting. Elks, who might be more intelligent than people give them credit for, seldom venture into clearings during the hunting season, but prefer to hide among the trees.

And there are many mushroom pickers who have simply given up – they are disappointed because 'their' forest has been clear-felled or, where they previously had their safe and top-secret spots, now they find a tightly planted young forest. They choose to buy their chanterelles in the market instead. So where will the witch in the gingerbread house live in future, she who is found in the deepest of all forests? And the troll? They are disturbed, of course, by the monotonous din of the forestry machines and can find nowhere to hide. Do we really want to have a forest where magic, beauty and culture is replaced with ranks of fir-tree corporals, planted with military precision?

# *Elks*

There are very many elks in Sweden. In the far north, in Överkalix, Korpilombolo, Boden and Råneå, there are around 17,000 of them, estimated by aerial counts. That means sixteen elks per thousand hectares. Forestry companies are not happy with the number of elks, because they chomp away at newly planted pines, their favourite winter food. In summer the entire elk population in Sweden is over 300,000 – but each year 100,000 animals are shot in the autumn elk hunt. The number of hunters is 300,000 and five per cent of them are women, a figure that seems to be increasing.

The elk hunt in Sweden is almost holy; it's a popular pastime for many, and even the king of Sweden takes part in the elk hunt on the mountains of Hunneberg and Halleberg and usually has his photograph taken, standing beside his slain quarry. It was a known truth in the past that the number of people off work sick rose sharply at the beginning of the elk-hunting season.

When the snow is more than fifty centimetres deep in the forests and fields, elks are tempted out onto the roads, where they can move around more easily. In 2011 it lay in a thick blanket over the whole of the country; it was a bitterly cold winter, and the temperature barely ever crept above zero in central Sweden during January and February. At the beginning of February my daughter and I were in the car on the road from Stockholm to Bohuslän. On the main roads the surface was dry; the sun shone over the white expanse; the fir trees looked as though they were dressed in white ball gowns – a beautiful, crisp winter land spread out around us. In Dalsland, about twenty-five kilometres from our destination, out of the corner of my eye I saw something looming up to our right, above a ditch; a huge elk, majestic and dignified, looked round, decided our car didn't represent a danger, stepped over the barbed wire enclosing some pastureland, and solemnly, on very long legs, walked out straight in front of the car, across the road and into the trees on the other side. I managed to brake and I could briefly see that an oncoming motorist avoided a collision with the animal by a hair's breadth too. We drove on, shaken by the incident, and I told my daughter that if she ever realised that hitting an elk was unavoidable, she should con- sciously aim for the animal's hindquarters, to prevent the long, kicking legs crashing in through the windscreen, something that would in all likelihood cause the driver's death.

Relieved and quite proud of keeping calm and not bursting into hysterical tears – we probably didn't have time to react, as it all happened so quickly – we continued our journey. The encounter with the elk, this primeval animal, seemed unreal and at the same time momentous, and we marvelled once again over the enormous size of an adult elk – it can be two metres and thirty centimetres tall to its shoulder and a bull elk can weigh up to 700 kilos. A little later, when I was approaching the crown of a hill, I had the sun in my eyes and could hardly see a thing; I didn't even have time to react when two elks sailed out right in front of the bumper. We could see another one standing by the forest, waiting. For the second time we'd escaped with our lives and reckoned that our elk quota for that day must have been well and truly met ... We drove on slowly, watching for more, but a third encounter was not to be.

Every year there are at least 5,000 accidents involving elks in Sweden – on that occasion we were lucky not to be one of the statistics. And so it is man, primarily as hunter, but also as motorist, who is the elk's main enemy, albeit packs of wolves hunt them too.

Elks are colour-blind – though I don't know how that can be established – and they have no great respect for cars, but on the other hand they do for people, whose smell they intensely dislike. In my mushroom forests I have met elks many times, deer too and once a lynx, foxes and badgers, of course, but regrettably never a wolf. Sometimes there is just the shadow of an elk that disappears, but I have also looked into an elk's eyes close up, and after a moment's silent understanding, we leave one another in peace. There is something awe-inspiring about meeting an elk on its own ground. Its gait is an expression of the landscape; the light movements are suited to tussocks in the bogs and labyrinthine passageways across the boulder fields. An elk doesn't exert itself, it flows through the landscape.

Germans are said to be especially fascinated by our Swedish elks – apparently they like to take away the signs that the Swedish Road Administration put at the side of the road to warn about elks, who often follow the same path at dawn or dusk to drink water from a particular stream. The sign, which has a picture of an elk on it, is made into a little table or hung on the wall. This is supposed to be true, and not just a popular Swedish myth. Another prevalent myth is that our national hero, Charles XII, commissioned Urban Hjärne and other experts to tame elks so they could be used as horses for the cavalry. This was unsuccessful, however ...

There are several elk parks in Sweden where the animals are kept in captivity and put on show for tourists – there's a sign near to us for Elk Café, for example, which could possibly be misinterpreted.

# Lakes without Sails

Discovering Lapland can be an overwhelming experience for a southern Swede. Is this really the same country you thought you knew because you'd been to Surte, Dingle, Västerfärnebo and Lund? Is that what a river looks like – like the Lule River or the Vindel River, not like the Kolbäcksån, Lagan, Nissan, Ätran or Viskan?

Travelling through Lapland changes all sense of proportion for someone from the south of Sweden; the world spreads out, empties of people, and becomes a forceful largo.

The rivers of southern Sweden are transformed into quiet streams compared to the Lule and the Vindel and the Torne, rivers as wide as lakes, once the means of transport for dead forests and now for enough megawatts to light up a whole city. Trees and hydropower are, together with the never-ending iron ore, the great export products from Norrland, the place that critical voices sometimes describe as being subject to colonial exploitation.

Everything here is slightly too big. A bog can continue, largely untouched by man or time, for 300 kilometres, the distance from Berlin to Hanover. Stunted birch trees, a long way apart, sudden glimpses of water, remarkable permafrost mounds like termite mounds, and all swathed in the apothecary smell of bogland plants, kilometre after kilometre.

But the most remarkable of all are the lakes. As imposing as inland seas, they lie, absolutely still, in the summer light: Storuman, Stora Lulevatten. Each covers an area of more than 160 square kilometres. (The vast expanse of the Åmänningen in northern Västmanland reaches a paltry 29 square kilometres.) At first glance these Lapland waters look like the great summer lakes we are accustomed to: the Mälaren, Vättern and Siljan. Until you suddenly notice the breathtaking difference.

*There are no boats.* Not a single boat as far as the eye can see. No marinas, no white sails, no motorboats creating a wash. For the first time in my life I am looking at lakes that have no boats in the summertime.

I realise that this is how lakes *actually* look. That boats are, in essence, a kind of graffiti on a pristine surface.

# Europe's Peaceful Attic

The best way of travelling to Europe's peaceful attic – the top part of inland Norrland – is with the Inlandsbanan. It is something of a miracle this railway line came into being at all and that it still exists – up to now it has survived every threat of closure. It is the last of all the illustrious railway construction in Sweden and tackling this project, intended to colonise the northern wilderness, caused immense hardship for all those who were involved.

That it is so important to preserve and develop this railway line is not just for their sake, even if it does feel as though the line should be kept out of sheer respect for the colossal labour it required. No, the line is and should continue in the future to be an essential transport route for people and goods between central and southern Sweden and Norrland's vast hinterland.

The Inlandsbanan, referred to in the 1905 edition of the *Nordic Family Book* as a project postponed after several parliamentary enquiries, was finally completed in 1937, and actually goes from Kristinehamn, by the great Lake Vänern in southern Sweden, right up to Gällivare in Lapland, above the

Arctic Circle, but the stretch from Kristinehamn to Mora has been closed. It could be reinstated if the municipalities concerned were interested, but at the moment it's not possible to board a train in Kristinehamn, as it was in the past, and travel the 1300 kilometres to Gällivare. However, it's entirely possible to get on at Mora, which lies at the point where the Dal River runs out into Lake Siljan, and set out from there on a great adventure. You can count on four or five days for this journey and you can decide in advance where along the line you will make your overnight stops and resume the following day. Inland Norrland is slowly being drained, as people move to the coast or to the south. It is sad to see such movement; the land you travel through is immensely beautiful and could so easily accommodate many more inhabitants and the infrastructure is still there. In large parts of the rest of Europe people are crowded together. The stations along the line, all individually designed, fit so well into the landscape. Have a look at them in Rolf Karbelius' book *Inlandsbanan: Fable and Reality*, with his affectionate and meticulous drawings and personal reflections on the buildings, landscape, history and people. The stations' exotic names, many of Sami origin, such as Vojmån, Tjappsåive, Varjisträsk and Kåbdalis, stimulate the imagination. Blattnicksele – doesn't it sound like a lost soul?

In Fågelsjö, a junction that was established long before the railway line was constructed, the train stops and a woman alights. A man is waiting for her outside the station building.

The man is rolling a cigarette as the woman steps over the tracks and they meet, fall into each other's arms, and stand motionless for a while. The train sets off slowly and leaves them to themselves. This short romantic film sequence is marred just a fraction by the woman handing the man a heavy plastic bag bearing the name Lidl.

Who were the people who toiled on this line through a land of wide lakes, huge rivers, beautiful forests rich with wild berries and mushrooms, the occasional farm that I'm glad to say is still in operation, boglands tens of kilometres wide, or boulders that look as though they've been tossed there by a giant, a wilderness you can hardly just wander around in? Those who carried out this type of heavy labour were called 'railroaders' and there is a host of stories about them, in both oral and written tradition. Let me cite the artist Rolf Karbelius, in his commentary on the aforementioned Fågelsjö junction:

> The railway builders toiled through an almost
> impenetrable wilderness, they heaved and hauled and
> hacked, they battered and blasted. They transported, laid
> out and secured the rails, they gravelled the embankments
> and carried on; their singing faded, only to be heard again
> in new parishes, over bogs and marshes, through valleys
> and over rivers. The railroaders left behind them a route
> for the arrival of a new civilisation, with neat stations,
> halts and regenerated communities. Whole new places
> grew up. Pearls were threaded on a string of steel uniting

the country and creating a new sense of solidarity between the two ends. It let the fresh air in and opened up the world.

An historical railway photograph shows a group of railroaders in their slouch hats carrying an eight-metre-long rail track over the bog on a path consisting of a narrow plank, a footbridge. The slightest stumble would be disastrous, the suction of the bog bottomless. It's hard to imagine the hardships these men suffered; they laboured in rain-soaked clothes in the first snows of October, or sweated in a cloud of mosquitoes in the month of June. They lived in barracks, always with a cook who looked after their food, separated in their dormitory for the sake of delicacy by a curtain. The cooks were skilful, proud working women, at a time when working women were not common, and they were warmly appreciated by the railroaders. The mere existence of the women in this markedly masculine environment must have made these men, some of them rough, to say the least, behave in a decent manner.

Suddenly there's a slight jolt, and the train slows down, stops and starts to go backwards. At the side of the track is a very dead elk. The driver doesn't seem to take it too seriously, just rings a representative of the hunt in this area and drives on. One of the reindeer running along the track meets the same fate.

There are aspects of this journey that exceed human comprehension. In one section a 160-kilometre bog stretches out, almost inaccessible in summertime, wetlands smelling of aromatic plants, as far as the horizon, where Sweden's highest mountain, Kebnekaise, appears like a faint, dark-blue shadow. This bog landscape, with its flocks of yellowhammers that suddenly fly up into the sky, its open water here and there, and its solitary birch trees standing forlorn, has an inimitable aura of melancholy and innocence. This is the land of Sami shamanism, the *noaidi*. And in ancient times, anthropologists tell us, giving yourself up to the bog was not an unusual way to die, for elderly Sami people who felt they were no longer able to take part in the task of reindeer herding and the seasonal movements every spring and autumn. In traditional Sami religion, choosing to die was an acknowledged prospect, it was not forbidden as it is in the Christian faith as a form of 'murder'. Here, on a July day, can you feel the temptation? To go further and further out into the supernatural stillness of the never-ending bog, to let yourself slowly sink into the brown, sun-warmed mossy water?

About the ring moving between the symbols on the drums, about the fishing practices and the dwellings, about Charles XI's tax collectors, the *birkarls* as they were called, about silver smithing and architecture, about boats and reindeer sleighs, about all of this and much more, we can learn a great deal in one of Northern Europe's richest and best organised ethnographic museums, the Sami museum in Jokkmokk.

The Sami people who live in these regions are not always surrounded by huge, steaming herds of reindeer, even if the local high schools do provide a course in reindeer husbandry intended for these cowboys of the North, now equipped with two-way radios and fast snow scooters. The truth is that the nomadic lifestyle has been abandoned. The taxi driver who takes you to the airport or the dental nurse who asks you to sit in the chair might have Sami origins. There is much to suggest that these remarkable people, the country's native inhabitants, who have been affected to a shameful extent by a mixture of negligence and paternalism on the part of Sweden's central authorities, are in fact heading into a new age and with new self-confidence and historical awareness. The outstanding museum in Jokkmokk bears witness to this.

There are different views on the Sami people's future. Reindeer herding endures in more modern forms; the eternal legal battle with the Swedish state about reindeer husbandry rights has, thanks to the sobering influence of the European Union, forced the traditional centralism of the Swedish state, a living relic from the time of Gustav Vasa and the Lutheran reformation, to take a few hesitant steps backwards for the first time.

For the last few years Swedish television has broadcast a daily news programme in Sami. We have to admit that we seldom miss this programme. Partly it's for the experience of a magical foreign language, in which we can only manage to distinguish a few words related to geographic realities: *sel* (calm water), *luokta* (bay) and *jaure* (lake). Partly it's to see the weather map in a whole new perspective. Norwegian, Swedish, Finnish and Russian Lapland form a single unit where the snowstorms are sweeping in; the world's southern border is somewhere down by Östersund.

Listening to these news broadcast, which could just as well have come from another country, a republic of great rivers and great empty lakes, it's easy to start worrying about the future of Sami culture. That Sami people will thrive is beyond all doubt. They were here before us and it's possible they'll be here after us. But Sami culture, this fascinating culture of survival over many thousands of years, with the peat huts, fishing tools, means of foretelling future events, the drum and its sharply reduced image of the known and manageable world, the ornaments and jewellery, boats that had young birch trees for sails in the spring migration – is all this to be reduced to a museum experience?

The brightly coloured Sami market in Jokkmokk, the happy, whirling dance with which it's celebrated, and the work of new Sami poets are interesting signs of a movement in the opposite direction.

At Moskosel the train halts and passengers are served an old Swedish dish of dumplings made from raw mashed or grated potatoes, mixed with flour and salt into a dough, and formed into round balls that are filled with pork. The balls are then boiled in salted water – and they are really very good! They are served with lingonberry preserve and melted butter and a lingonberry juice to drink with it.

To some degree it's possible for a few people to remain here running small businesses based around the tourist industry the railway line has brought with it. One couple, originally from Denmark, have made a brave move, leaving the relative security of home to run a restaurant and shop at one of the stations, which is fortunately also on the road. A Sami is offering reindeer skins (much cheaper than in the souvenir shops), reindeer sausages, cloudberry preserve and Sami art right on the Arctic Circle, where several of the passengers feel the need to be photographed.

At Gällivare, over 1,300 kilometres from Stockholm, in other words further from Stockholm than Berlin is, our journey ends. We alight at the huge wooden station and see the iron ore wagons that travel between Luleå and Narvik in Norway go thundering past, heavily laden, and not just occasionally, but at least one an hour. This is the artery that will end in the steelworks of Japan and motor industry of China. In Gällivare and Kiruna there are large, extremely profitable iron ore mines, Europe's largest copper mine and Aitik, Sweden's biggest gold mine. Some of them are or have been opencast mines. The giant funnel-shaped crater we see from the plane on the way home has the same architecture as Dante's Inferno, with concentric ledges or 'benches', where lorries that are said to be bigger and more terrifying than any on the road are driven only by women. Presumably for the same reason that the core engineers, round, harmonious civil engineers in the Forsmark nuclear power plant, often with some knitting on their knees, are women. Women are regarded for some reason as less likely to be distracted by sudden urges. An ore truck in a skid would of course be a huge disaster; it would fall from one level to the next, right down into the narrow centre, where in Dante's parallel world Satan would cheerily eat a few of the chosen sinners.

It is when the large Arctic mines change from opencast to drift mining that the real problems begin. The fact is that Kiruna, with its schools, churches and housing, is being swallowed up by its mine and within the next few years will have to be moved to safer ground. That this project is not just seen as realistic, but is also going to be implemented, says something about the enormous financial resources an iron ore quarry such as this one can mobilise.

It's a shame that the little shanty town in Malmberget, which resembles a Klondike from the beginning of the twentieth century, with its narrow streets and striking shops, is also going to disappear. The blocks of flats at the nearest bus stop are already empty, the shop windows boarded up with plywood. Signposts to the underworld, you might say, in the words of the poet Gunnar Ekelöf.

If you happen to get off the train in Gällivare on a Friday evening and take a room in the big hotel opposite the station, with the spectacular view over the lake and mountain, you will witness something genuinely Swedish. We don't really understand why there are six beefy guards outside the still sparsely occupied dining room, where, after our rail journey adventure, we are enjoying a seafood cocktail, beer, snaps, exquisitely cooked reindeer meat, and cloudberry ice cream. But soon the picture clears. One man after another saunters into the hotel, not exactly fashionably dressed in their checked shirt and trousers with the 'Gällivare hang' – a far cry from the sophisticated clientele in the bars around Stureplan in Stockholm. As they stand at the bar and order one beer and chaser after another, it becomes obvious that we are not the target audience this evening. They seem to want us out of the way; our table is cleared of plates and glasses unusually quickly. The first pretty girls turn up, meticulously made-up and dressed, but they are in a distinct minority. The atmosphere becomes increasingly tense. Any girl at all can pick and choose here ... We just say: Good luck!

Eventually the music is too loud for our ears and we retire to our room. We watch with interest as the police cars glide around among the youths who have left the bar or are coming back. We see loneliness, drunkenness and brawls. But we also see couples happily embracing as they walk out into the almost ethereal light of the summer's night.